Heavenly Horizons 365 Biblical Bedtime Stories for Young Hearts, 2-in-1 Value Pack

Discover God's Wonders in the New and Old Testaments with Questions and Prayers for Kids Ages 4–8. Biblical Bedtime Stories for Kids BIBLICAL BEDTIME STORIES FOR KIDS Only One Life

Only One Life

Contents

Biblical Bedtime Stories for Kids

New Testament Amazing Moments Pointing Your Children to God; Ages 4 - 8.

Only One Life

Only One Life

Contents

INTRODUCTION

Hey, so glad you're here. God has so much to share
• • • with us about who He is, and how much He loves us
and wants to connect with us.

This book of Biblical stories is standalone. But when com-
bined with the 'Biblical Bedtime Stories for Kids... Old Testament Amazing Moments; Pointing Your Children to God,'
you will have 365 days of either stories or prayers that will
take each family through an entire year of walking with
God.

I made a corresponding coloring book, '... New Testament
Amazing Moments; Pointing Your Children To God Coloring Book', to go with the stories from this book. The coloring book is sold separately or you can download it for free
from onlyonelifestory.com and will reinforce the teachings
to help your kids understand, visualize, and retain what is in
this book. The Old Testament Storybook also has a coloring
book to go along with it for easy visualization and hands-on
for the children. You can also buy or download it from the
same website.

This book, on its own, will take each family through 165
days of walking with God in the New Testament. The aim
is for parents to read one prayer or story per day and use
this as a basis for teaching their children about God - who

He is, what He is like, His relationship with humanity, and His moral rules for everyday living.

This book brings us the New Testament truths about Jesus and His teachings. God Almighty has a plan for us, our families, and everyone in the world from the very beginning of creation.

My thought for each family is a story or a prayer each day. **Children learn well when stories are repeated.** Because of that, I decided to write the book to alternate with either a story or a prayer, so parents can use the days of prayer to return to the story and retell it in their way or reread the story before the prayer. I wrote the prayers to encourage children to pray and praise God, show them how to express their feelings, and talk to Him as a trusted Father. The prayers are linked to the Bible stories and focus on their lessons.

In this book, we will use the most powerful name — **Jesus** — in our prayer lives. We will be thankful to God because He has said in His Word that we should be grateful in every situation. We will learn about the birth of our Lord Jesus Christ, how Satan tempted Him, and teachings from Him. We will also know how Peter prayed and raised Dorcas from death. Oh, also Paul–how he troubled the followers of Jesus Christ and eventually became one himself.

Central to the writing of this book is the belief that all humans are sinners that need a Savior and that there is only one way to our salvation–through faith in Jesus Christ, God's Son. Some people may view the stories as moral teachings, which no doubt they are. Still, the main reason I wrote this book rests on believing that both children and adults need the Savior. That is because I know, "*That if you confess with your mouth the Lord Jesus and believe in your heart that God has raised Him from the dead, you will be saved,"* Romans 10:9. Praise God! It doesn't matter if they are young. The Lord wants hearts that will believe in Him and a mouth that will confess Him.

I pray "that God will give you the spirit of wisdom and revelation in the knowledge of Him, that He will open the eyes of your understanding that you may know the hope of His calling, the riches of His glory, and the greatness of His power towards you, according to the working of His power, which He worked in Christ, when He raised Him from the dead," (Ephesians 1:17-20). In Jesus' name. Amen!

Day 1 - Zachariah Hears Some Good News

G od was all set to send His Son into the world. Nobody in Israel knew when and how this would happen. But He had promised the Israelites, His people, that He would send a special messenger first. This person would prepare the people to receive His Son when He arrived. So, they patiently waited for God to keep His promise.

This is what happened. There was a priest named Zachariah (or Zechariah or Zacharias). This priest and his wife, Elizabeth, had no children and kept praying for one. One day, while he was in the temple, an angel appeared to him suddenly. Zechariah, the priest, was afraid, but the angel told him not to be scared because God had heard his prayer. He would have a son and was to name him John.

How would you feel if you were Zachariah and heard this? He should have been pleased about this. But was he?

Day 2 - Prayer

God, I thank You so much because I know You always want to bless me.

Help me listen to You for instructions on what to do so You can bless me. I can't wait to receive another blessing from You. Thank You for Your many blessings. In Jesus' name. Amen.

Day 3 - Zachariah Does Not Believe God

An angel told Zachariah that he was going to have a son. He should have been happy because he always asked God to give him one. But maybe because he had been asking for such a long time, he did not believe what the angel told him.

So, he asked the angel, "How can this happen, for I am an old man?"

Then the angel said, "I am Gabriel who stands before God in Heaven. He sent me here to tell you this good news. But because you do not believe me, you will not be able to speak from now until the day the child is born."

Zechariah was frightened. I am sure he wished he had believed what the angel had told him. Now it was too late. We should never doubt God when He speaks His Words to us through the Bible.

Do you believe everything your parents tell you?

What is one thing the Bible says that you find hard to believe?

Day 4 - Zachariah Cannot Speak

The angel told Zachariah that he would not be able to speak until after his son was born. Zachariah must have been frightened and wondered if this was true. He soon found out because when he came out of the room in the temple, the people spoke to him, but he found out that he could not talk back to them. It happened the way the angel had said. He was now unable to speak with his mouth. He felt so ashamed. He could not wait to finish his work at the temple. As soon as he finished, he hurried back to his home in the country.

What would you do if you were Zachariah?

How would you feel?

I am sure he felt sorry for not believing God's message. Now he would be dumb for about nine months. That is a very long time.

We will find out what happens in the following story.

Day 5 - Prayer

T hank You, God, for being with me wherever I go. Dear God, help me believe Your Word when I hear or read it. Let me not doubt You because I can't see You.

My Father, I know that You are always with me, and what Your Word says is true. Give me an obedient heart that hears and quickly believes Your Word. Thank You for the Word You speak to me every day from the Bible. In Jesus' name. Amen.

Day 6 - Zachariah's Wife Expects a Baby

Zachariah hurried home from his work in the temple. He could not speak, and he had to tell his wife, Elizabeth, why. Maybe he talked to her using his hands to make signs or wrote them down. She must have been shocked to find out why he could not speak. Then one day, Elizabeth found out that she would have a baby. Now Zachariah knew that what God said was true. He was going to have the son he had always wanted. His unborn son would be a unique child, making it even more interesting. The angel had said that his unborn son, John, would make many of his people accept the Savior when He came. He was to be God's messenger to them to tell them about His Son, Jesus Christ, who would soon come to earth. That was terrific news, and God used Zachariah and Elizabeth to make this happen.

You should never forget that God uses people like you and me to do His work.

Do you know God created you with a purpose, just like John and Jesus?

Day 7 - Prayer

F ather, I am so glad that You use ordinary people like me to do Your work on earth.

I am so grateful for that. Zachariah was doing his job in the temple; his wife was doing her work at home, and when You were ready to send Your prophet, John, into the world, You chose them as his parents. Please help me keep doing the right things, and You should use me when You know I am ready to take up the task you planned for me. Thank You for having a solid plan for my life. In Jesus' name. Amen.

Day 8 - Zachariah's Son is Born

Zachariah and Elizabeth were pleased they were going to have a son. For the nine months of Elizabeth's pregnancy, Zachariah could not speak. At last, the day came when the baby was born. Everyone wanted to know what his parents were going to call him. In those days, people named their babies after their fathers or someone else from the family. Everyone expected Zachariah would do the same thing. But when the time of the baby's naming arrived, they asked his mother what the child's name was, for she was the one that could talk. She told them his name was John.

"But nobody in your whole family has that name," they said. Curious about what Zachariah might say, they answered, "Let's ask the child's father."

Zachariah could not speak still, so he asked for something to write on. Everyone waited eagerly to see what he was going to write. Would he call him John, as the angel had told him to? Zachariah knew the child was to be someone special. He also wanted to obey God. So, he wrote the word, 'JOHN,' which became the baby's name.

And guess what? As soon as he did this, he could speak, just like the angel had told him.

I am sure Zechariah was glad to be able to talk again. Wouldn't you be?

If you were Zachariah, apart from just being happy to talk, what else would you have done?

Day 9 - Prayer

T hank You, God, for giving me to my parents just like You gave John to his family. Help me become the person You want me to be when I grow up. Thank You for making me special. In Jesus' name. Amen.

Day 10 - Zachariah Praises God for His Baby Boy

Zachariah named his baby boy John, just as the angel had told him to some months before. After writing that his name should be John, he could suddenly talk again. The first thing Zachariah did was praise God. He blessed God for sending him a son whom he wanted so much. He also thanked Him for making his son, John, a special messenger of Israel's soon-coming Savior. Zachariah no longer doubted God because everything the angel had told him had come true.

We should not doubt God's messages to us in the Bible.

Do you know the Bible is God's message to you?

How seriously do you take the teachings from the Bible?

Day 11 - Prayer

I praise You, my Father, for making babies like me and letting us grow up. Thank You for giving me to my parents. They take good care of me all the time, and they love me very much. It makes me so happy. Thank You for loving me, dear God. In Jesus' name. Amen.

Day 12 - An Angel Visits Mary

Before John was born, an angel visited a young woman named Mary. She was a cousin of Elizabeth, Zachariah's wife, who is the mother of John. Like John's father, God gave the angel a message for Mary. The angel told Mary that God chose her to have a special baby. The angel instructed her to give the child the name Jesus because He would save His people from their sins. He was also going to be the Son of God and the Savior promised to Israel long ago.

You see..., God had promised His people that He would send them someone to save them from their enemies. Many years had passed, and the promised Savior had not come. Now, God was about to send Him into the world.

God will always do as He promised, even if it takes a long time.

What have your parents promised you that you have been waiting to receive?

How much do you trust them to fulfill their promise to you?

Do you enjoy waiting for so long?

What can you do to calm yourself down when waiting for something?

Day 13 - Prayer

Thank You, dear God, for always keeping Your promises. Let me always remember this. You kept Your promise to Israel, and I know You will also keep Your promises to me. Please, help me keep my promises to You and my fellow human beings so that I will be like You. Thank You for making that happen. In Jesus' name. Amen.

Day 14 - Mary and the Angel

M ary felt very afraid when she saw the angel, and she was even more worried when he told her she would have a baby. But, unlike Zachariah, Mary believed what the angel said. How do I know this? I know from her reply to the angel.

After the angel gave her God's message, Mary said, "Let it happen to me as God has said."

Mary believed God right there and accepted what the angel said. We all should be more like her, quick to believe what God tells us all the time.

Do you constantly doubt what your parents tell you or always believe them?

How do you feel when you tell someone the truth and the person disbelieves you?

Day 15 - Mary Visits Elizabeth

The angel did not only tell Mary that she would have a baby boy. He also said to her that Elizabeth, her cousin, would also have a child. Mary hurried to visit her cousin in the hill country. A strange thing happened when Mary entered the house and greeted Elizabeth. The baby in Elizabeth's tummy jumped up and down. That sometimes happens to women who are expecting a baby. You might have done it, too! Ask your mother.

The two cousins were happy to see each other and shared their stories about the angel's visits and the children they were going to have. The two of them knew their babies would be extra special. They praised and thanked God for His kindness to them.

Hmm..., do you always praise God for making you unique?

What are some things you always praise God for?

Have you ever praised God for giving you free air to breathe?

Day 16 - Prayer

God, I want to thank You for my mother. She is so kind, loving, and good to me. Every day, she takes excellent care of me. She does many things to make me happy. Thank You for her, God. In Jesus' name. Amen.

Day 17 - No Room in the Inn

Mary returned home and lived with her husband, Joseph, in Nazareth. It was nearly time for her to have baby Jesus. Joseph had to go to Bethlehem for a census, so he took Mary with him. When they arrived in Bethlehem, there were lots of people. They had all come for the same reason, so the town was very crowded. Joseph tried very hard to find a room in an inn for them to stay in. He knew the baby was coming soon, but everywhere was full. There was no room in any of the inns for them.

Where were they to go? Where would baby Jesus be born?

Will you be scared if you are traveling, your parents did not find a hotel, and you all have to sleep in the car in the middle of nowhere?

Will you be scared to hear the howling of the wolves and coyotes? What about the hooting of the owls?

Day 18 - Prayer

Lord God, thank You for the birth of baby Jesus. I am sorry that no one wanted to let Mary into their house. It must have made her sad. But thank You, God, for taking care of her, Joseph, and baby Jesus that night. Help me be kind to people who need my help. Thank You very much for baby Jesus. In Jesus' name. Amen.

Day 19 - Jesus is Born

In Bethlehem, Joseph and Mary could not find a place to stay the night, and he had to find one because Mary might soon have her baby. The only place they could find was in a stable with animals.

That night, Mary had her baby. She clothed Him in pieces of cloth and put Him in a manger to sleep. Jesus, the Son of God, was born in a stable and slept in a manger. That was something that animals eat their food from. He was not born in a castle where kings lived. He was born like a poor person, although He was God's Son. That tells us it does not matter where you are born because God is everywhere and with us always.

Have you ever asked your mom to tell you where you were born?

Were you born in a hospital, house, or barn?

Day 20 - Prayer

Thank You, God, for sending Jesus as a baby. Let me remember He is Your Christmas gift to us. I happily receive Him into my heart so that He will be with me forever. Thank You, dear Jesus, for coming into the world to be my Savior. In Jesus' name. Amen.

Day 21 - The Angels and Shepherds Celebrated Jesus' Birth

The very night Jesus was born, there were many shepherds in the field. They were watching over their sheep to keep them safe. Suddenly, an angel appeared to one group of these shepherds. The place became very bright, and the shepherds were afraid. The angel told the shepherds not to be scared. He was bringing them some very good news. Then he said to them that Jesus, the Son of God, who is the promised Savior, had just been born. He told them where He was and that they would find Him wrapped in pieces of cloth and lying in a manger.

What would you do if someone told you this?

Would you think you are dreaming?

Day 22 - Prayer

I am so glad, Father, that Jesus was born. I want to sing with the angels about Him coming to earth. I want to clap my hands, stomp my feet and shout out the wonderful good news. Hurrah! Jesus Christ, our Savior, is born! God, Thank You for sending Him to us in Jesus' name. Amen.

Day 23 - The Shepherds Visit Baby Jesus

T he angel just told the shepherds that Jesus, the Savior God had promised to Israel, was born and where to find Him. That was excellent news for them. Everyone in Israel knew of God's promise of a Savior. They had waited a very long time for it to happen. Now, at last, He was here.

So, the shepherds went and visit the baby. They wanted to see if what the angel had said was true. When they came to the manger, they found the baby and His parents. It was just like the angel told them. They were happy, and they praised God. Then they began telling everybody about this special child named Jesus. We should tell others about Jesus, God's Son and Savior of the World.

Who is the first person you will tell about Jesus, who died for the entire world?

Why is the birth of Jesus Christ good news for us?

Day 24 - Prayer

Come on, everybody, let us join with the shepherds and praise the Lord. Hallelujah! Praise the Lord! God has sent His only dear Son into the world. Let us receive Him with joy and gladness. Thank You, Lord, for your wonderful gift to us. In Jesus' name. Amen.

Day 25 - The Wise Men Follow a Star

In a faraway country lived some Wise Men. They were constantly studying the stars in the sky. They knew stars could tell stories about what God was doing. That was one reason why God had made them. But you had to be wise to know this. The Three Wise Men spent a lot of time studying the stars to see what they meant.

When Jesus was born, they saw a very bright new star in the sky. They knew it meant a special new King was born and pointed to where He was. So, they set out from their country to find this King. The star led them, and they followed it. Do you want to know where it took them?

Have you ever looked at the stars at night?

Do you see how wonderful God is when you look at the stars?

Day 26 - Prayer

Thank You, God, for Your good works in my life. The Wise Men came looking for Jesus, dear Father, because they knew He was special. I know He is special, too, so help me find Him, just like the Wise Men. Thank You again for the newborn King. In Jesus' name. Amen.

Day 27 - The Wise Men Find Jesus

The Wise Men from a far country in the East followed a bright star they saw in the sky. They knew it was telling them about the birth of a unique King. So, they set out to find Him. They packed lots of things for their long journey. They also took some gifts for this King. They journeyed for a very long time until they came to Jerusalem. They followed the star until it stopped over a house in Bethlehem. They found Mary, Joseph, and baby Jesus when they went inside. They knew Jesus was the King the star was telling them about. They bowed down, worshipped the Savior of the World, and gave Him three gifts—gold, frankincense, and myrrh.

If we are wise, we, too, should seek Jesus today. He is no longer a child, but He is still the Savior of the World.

The Wise Men gave Jesus gifts, and we should give Him a gift, too. God only wants one gift from us—our hearts. When we give Him our hearts, He will come in and live in it, like a house. How awesome!

To give Him your heart, you need to confess with your mouth the Lord Jesus and believe in your heart that God raised Him from the dead (Romans 10:9).

Now, are you ready to give Him your heart?

Day 28 - Prayer

God, I bow down and worship You because You are the only God. There is no God who is like You in the whole wide world. I am giving myself (heart) to You as a present. Let my heart be Your dwelling place as long as I live. Please help me keep following Jesus all of my life. Thank You that You are pleased when I give myself as a gift to You. In Jesus' name. Amen.

Day 29 - Simeon Blesses Baby Jesus

Mary and Joseph always tried to obey God. He told the people of Israel to take their children to the temple to be blessed a few days after birth. So, Mary and Joseph decided to do this. While Jesus' parents went to the temple, an older man met them. He was a righteous man named Simeon. He was always praying and doing whatever God told him to do. He came into the temple where the priest was blessing Jesus.

After the priest finished blessing baby Jesus, Simeon took baby Jesus in his arms. He, too, blessed baby Jesus and said He, Jesus, was sent from God to bring God's light and glory to all people. God loves to bless little children. Even Jesus took little children in His arms and blessed them. He has a special love for children like you.

I know you have seen lots of little children. Have you ever said something good about them?

Day 30 - Prayer

Lord God, I worship Your name for who You are. Father God, I know You love me. Bless me, I pray. Mary and Joseph obeyed Your rules by taking baby Jesus to the temple to be blessed. Lord, help my parents always to follow You, too. Please enable them to do what is right. Help them take me to church to hear Your Word since I cannot go on my own. Please remind them that You have given me to them to look after. Help them know their responsibility of teaching me Your ways. Thank You, God, for I know You have answered me. In Jesus' name. Amen.

Day 31 - Anna Blesses Baby Jesus, Too

Simeon was not the only person who blessed Jesus. An older woman, Anna, was living in the temple in Jerusalem. She prayed a lot, day and night. She came into the temple while the priest was blessing Jesus. When she saw Jesus, she knew He was the promised Savior, too. She praised and thanked God for sending Him.

The birth of Jesus made angels and people praise God. That is still a wonderful thing for us to do at Christmas and year long.

Have you praised God today?

What did you praise Him for?

Day 32 - Prayer

L et us praise God today.

Let us ring the bells, "Ring-a-ling!"

Let us beat the drum, "Boom! Boom!"

Let us blow our horns, "Toot! Toot!"

Jesus is getting a special blessing today.

Let us thank the Lord God for sending His Son, Jesus, to bless us.

In Jesus' name. Amen.

Day 33 - The Wise Men Meet Herod, the King

Herod was the King of Israel. He lived in Jerusalem. Before the Wise Men found Jesus in Bethlehem, they came to Jerusalem. They had followed the star and knew that it meant that the King of the Jews was born. But they were not yet sure of the exact place.

So, in Jerusalem, they asked, "Where is He who is born King of the Jews?"

King Herod heard about this and sent them to find out where this new king was. He asked the Wise Men about Him. They told Herod about the star they had followed and how it had led them to Israel. The Wise Men had come to worship the newborn King. Herod called some Jewish writers and asked them where it was said Jesus would be born in the Bible. They told him in Bethlehem, not too far from Jerusalem. Herod then asked the Wise Men to find Jesus, come back, and tell him when they did.

He told the Wise Men, "I want to worship King Jesus, too."

Do you believe him?

Day 34 - Prayer

Lord, I want to bow down and worship the King, Jesus Christ, who is Your Son. You sent Him into the world as a gift for us. Thank You for this beautiful gift. In Jesus' name. Amen.

Day 35 - God Warns the Wise Men Not to Go Back to Herod

The Wise Men promised to let King Herod know when they found baby Jesus. They traveled to Bethlehem, where they saw Jesus and His parents. They worshipped Him because He was the Son of God and gave Him their gifts. Then they remembered that King Herod had said he wanted to worship Jesus, too. They had promised to tell him where they found Jesus. They thought of going back to Jerusalem to let Herod know this, but an angel, in a dream, warned them not to do this. So, they left Bethlehem and returned to their country on another road.

Why did God tell the Wise Men not to return to King Herod?

Do you think God was right to tell the Wise Men not to return to Herod?

Day 36 - King Herod Tries to Kill Baby Jesus

God told the Three Wise Men not to go back to tell King Herod about finding Jesus. The king waited for them to return. When they did not come back, he realized they had tricked him. He became furious. So, he sent his soldiers to Bethlehem. He told them to kill every boy baby two years old and under. He did not want Jesus to become King of the Jews, and he tried to stay king for as long as he could. The soldiers killed many babies, and this made their families sad.

Did the soldiers kill Jesus?

How do you think the parents of the babies Herod killed felt?

Day 37 - Prayer

Thank You, God, for keeping baby Jesus safe so He could grow up to be a big man. Joseph and Mary must have been very happy they were safe from Herod's soldiers. Thank You, dear Lord, for always watching over us. In Jesus' name. Amen.

Day 38 - God Tells Joseph to Leave Bethlehem

G od knows everything before it happens. That is why we must always listen to Him and obey what He says. He knew King Herod wanted to kill Jesus. So, before the king sent his soldiers to Bethlehem to kill the boy babies, the angel of God spoke to Joseph in a dream. He told him to take Jesus and His mother and run to Egypt because King Herod wanted to kill the newborn King. Joseph believed God, and so he took his family to Egypt. That was why King Herod did not kill Jesus.

It is a good thing always to obey God.

Do you always find it difficult to obey your parents?

Why?

Day 39 - Prayer

Thank You, God, for always watching over me. Thank You for the guardian angels You send to keep me safe all the time. Thank You for always taking me home safely every day I left. Thank You for being my Father in Heaven. In Jesus' name. Amen.

Day 40 - Jesus is Lost in Jerusalem

After King Herod died, God told Joseph to return to Israel. He, Mary, and Jesus went to live in Nazareth.

Every year, Jesus' family went up to the temple in Jerusalem at a particular time to worship God. When Jesus was twelve years old, Jesus and His family went up to the temple as usual. After spending a few days in Jerusalem's temple, it was time to go home.

Mary and Joseph had lots of friends with them, so they thought Jesus was in their crowd as they were returning home. But along the way, they looked for Jesus and could not find Him. They were very worried, and so they hurried back to Jerusalem. It took Jesus' parents three days to find Him.

Where did they find Jesus?

Do you always like to stay in your parents' company or your friends when you are in the park? Why?

Day 41 - Prayer

Heavenly Father and my God, I want to thank You for always being with us all the time. It must have been scary for Jesus' parents not to know where He was. But they went to the right place—Your house. That is a perfect place to be, and Jesus must have felt safe. Thank You, Lord, for taking care of us when we are lost. In Jesus' name. Amen.

Day 42 - Jesus is Found

When Jesus' parents saw Him, He was in the temple talking with some older people about the Word of God. His parents were upset because He had not come along with them. His mother asked Him why He had stayed behind because they had been worried about Him. Jesus told her He was not lost, but He was doing His Father's business. He meant His Father, God, not Joseph.

You know..., even if we have our earthly father, we still have a Father in Heaven, too. Like us, Jesus had an earthly father and a Heavenly Father. Our Heavenly Father cares so much for us. We should always talk to Him the way we speak to our earthly father.

Learning God's Word was very important to Jesus. He did not mean to be rude or hurt His parents. He was just so busy learning the Word of God that He did not remember going home. Just like Jesus, we should do everything we can to learn the Word of God because it gives life.

After they found Him, Jesus went home with His parents and was obedient to them.

What are your favorite coloring works? Are they about random kinds of stuff or the Bible?

Visit us at support@onlyonelifestory.com to receive a pdf copy you can print out to keep your kids engaged.

Day 43 - Prayer

God, I want to praise You for giving me parents that love me. Help me obey my parents, just like Jesus did. I know they love me and want the best for me. Let me not say unkind things to them or give them too much trouble. I worship Your name again. In Jesus' name. Amen.

Day 44 - John the Baptizer

While Jesus was growing into a man, His cousin, John the Baptist, was also becoming a man. But he lived in the wilderness and only ate locusts and wild honey as food.

Oooh, yummy or yucky?

Before John was born, God had told his father that John would be a messenger for Jesus. That meant that John's job was to tell people about Jesus before Jesus started His ministry. This way..., they would be ready to receive Jesus into their hearts when He comes.

It was now time for John to do this. So, one day, John began preaching about Jesus, the Savior they each needed. He told the people to get ready for Jesus because His coming was near.

We, too, must tell others about Jesus. We are now His messengers to tell everybody that Jesus is coming again and that His coming is very near. Are you ready to tell people what you know about Jesus?

What would you say about Him if I asked you to tell me about Jesus right now?

Day 45 - Prayer

F ather, I praise You for promising that Jesus will come
for us again. We know the coming of Jesus is near
because Your Word says so. Like John, help us get ourselves
ready and tell others, so they might be prepared to meet
Jesus when He arrives. Again, I praise Your holy name, O
God. In Jesus' name. Amen.

Day 46 – Jesus Comes to be Baptized

John kept on preaching about the coming of Jesus. He told them to prepare their hearts by turning from the wrong things they were doing. He also told them to be baptized. Many Jews came to the River Jordan, where John was preaching. Some of them turned from their sins and were baptized. Then one day, Jesus went to the river so that John could baptize Him. John was very surprised because Jesus did not have any sin. He was the Son of God, and God does not sin. John did not want to baptize Jesus, but Jesus said He had to be baptized because this was what God wanted all His followers to do. So, John baptized Jesus in the River Jordan. That day, something amazing happened.

Can you guess what happened?

Day 47 - Prayer

Thank You, Father, for sending Jesus to teach us to obey Your Word. He is Your Son, and He knew He should obey You. Teach us to be like Him—obedient to You and our earthly parents. I adore You for always being with us and helping us all the way. In Jesus' name. Amen.

Day 48 – God Shows that Jesus is Very Special

J esus went to His cousin John so he would baptize Him. John baptized Him in the River Jordan. As Jesus emerged from the water, Heaven opened, and John saw something like a dove fly down from Heaven, and it rested on top of Jesus.

Then he heard a voice saying, "This is my beloved Son who pleases me very well."

That was God speaking. Oh wow!

Now John knows Jesus is the Son of God who came down from Heaven to earth. We must believe this, too, and welcome Him into our hearts.

What does that dove represent?

Day 49 - Prayer

Dear God in Heaven, I lift Your name on high because You made me special. That is why You sent Your only beloved Son, Jesus, to die for me. Because You did this, I know You love me very much. I want to say thank You for loving me so much. I want to spend all my life loving You back for Your goodness to me. Thank You for Your greatness. In Jesus' name. Amen.

Day 50 – Satan and Jesus

D id you know God has an enemy who hates Him? Yes, and his name is Satan. He wants to take over the world from God and rule it. He does not want to obey God, who created him, or do anything God tells him to do. He is evil. Satan tries to hurt people all the time and wants us to hurt each other. But more than anything, he wants us to disobey God. That makes him happy. So, he is always trying to make us sin. Do you want to know what he did to Jesus? He tried to make Him disobey God.

Did Satan make Jesus sin?

Day 51 - Prayer

Dear God, I am so happy whenever I remember how you smashed Satan for my sake. Please help me believe that Satan exists. I sometimes wonder if he is real because I can't see Him. But if he came and tempted Jesus, then he must be real. Please teach me how to deal with him so that I will not fall into his trap. Help me believe and I praise You, Lord, for giving me power over him. In Jesus' name. Amen.

Day 52 - Satan's First Test for Jesus

S atan wanted Jesus to disobey God, His Father, so he came to Jesus in the desert after John baptized Him. There he tempted Jesus three times to do something wrong. First, Satan told Jesus that He should turn some stones into bread if He were indeed the Son of God.

Of course, Jesus could do this and much more because He is the Son of God. Jesus was all alone, tired, and very hungry because He had not eaten for forty days and nights.

But should He?

No.

Why?

Because we must do nothing Satan tells us to do. So, Jesus did not listen to him. Jesus passed the first test.

Do you know Satan always tells the children of God to do wrong things every day?

What are some things that Satan always wants people to do?

Day 53 - Prayer

Our Father in Heaven, thank You for always being with me. Please keep me safe from the devil when he comes to tempt me to do wrong. Please assist me in being like Jesus and saying, "No!" to Satan all the time. Thank You, Lord, for giving me power over him. In Jesus' name. Amen.

Day 54 - Satan's Second Test for Jesus

J esus passed the first test from Satan. So, Satan tried to get Jesus to sin in another way. He took Jesus way up to the top of the Temple in Jerusalem. Then he told Jesus that if He were indeed the Son of God, He should throw Himself down from there. Satan even reminded Him that the Bible said God would save Him from falling if something like that happens. That was true, but only if Jesus was not falling to show off. So, Jesus told Satan, "No!" again and did not obey him.

Wow! Jesus won over Satan two times now.

Will He win the last time?

What would you have done if you were Jesus?

Day 55 - Prayer

God, You are so wonderful. You gave us the Holy Bible, filled with how we can live and know all Satan's tricks. Please assist me in understanding what the Bible says, so Satan does not trick me into doing the wrong thing. Thank You for my parents and the writer of this book, helping me understand what You want me to know from the Bible so that I can be safe. In Jesus' name. Amen.

Day 56 - Satan's Last Test for Jesus

J esus had passed Satan's test two times. Satan certainly was not happy. He kept on losing, as Jesus would not obey him. He decided to try one last thing. He knew people liked to be rich, famous, and have lots of power. Maybe he could get Jesus to sin in one of these areas. So, he offered Jesus all the riches and control of the world. But guess what? Satan said Jesus would have to worship him before he could have those things.

Can you believe that? Was Satan the true God of the entire world? Did he make everything and give life to everyone?

No!

Jesus knew this, and so did Satan. So, Jesus said, "No!" one last time. Then Satan left Him shamefully because he knew he could not make Him disobey God.

Hurray for Jesus! He won!

We should be like Jesus, only obeying God and never Satan.

Has Satan ever tempted you before?

How did you know it was Satan?

Day 57 - Prayer

T hank You, God, that Jesus passed all the tests. Thank You, He did not let Satan win. Teach me to obey Your Word, so I, too, will pass the test when Satan tempts me to do wrong. Thank You for Your Word is powerful. In Jesus' name. Amen.

Day 58 - Jesus Chooses His Disciples

After the temptations, Jesus came back from the desert. He began to preach that the Kingdom of God was soon to come. Many people started following Him to hear what He had to say. One of the first people to follow Jesus was Andrew. He was a follower of John the Baptist. One day, he heard John say of Jesus, "Look at the Lamb of God, who takes away the world's sins!"

Andrew wanted to know what John meant by referring to Jesus as 'the Lamb of God who takes away the world's sins.' So, he began following Jesus. After a little while, he asked Jesus where He lived, and Jesus invited him to come and see. From that day, Andrew became a follower of Jesus.

Why did people follow Jesus? They wanted to know Him better and to become like Him. Jesus still invites us to follow Him today. Will you? What makes the followers of Jesus separate from the rest people?

Day 59 - Prayer

Precious Father, I want to praise You for choosing me to be Your child. I want to follow You all the days of my life to know You better. May You show me how You want me to go, so I can keep following You. Thank You for I know You have answered me. In Jesus' name. Amen.

Day 60 - More Disciples Follow Jesus

We call people who followed Jesus when He was on earth His disciples. Today, we call them Christians. Many other people followed Jesus in His time and became His disciples. He had twelve special disciples who went with Him everywhere. After becoming a disciple, Andrew went and called his brother, Peter.

James and John were brothers, too. Jesus called them to be His disciples while they were in their father's boat on the sea, fishing. They left everything and followed Him. Jesus also called Philip, who invited Nathanael to come along because they *"have found Him of whom Moses in the law, and also the prophets, wrote—Jesus of Nazareth, the son of Joseph."* Matthew was a tax collector, and Jesus also called him to be His disciple, and he came along.

Jesus called other people, but some were too busy, some did not want to leave what they had, and some were just not interested. Those who answered His call to become disciples were the wise ones. Do you want to be a Christian, to get to know Jesus?

Remember, Jesus called all kinds of people, even children. He said, "Let the little children come to me..." (Mathew 19:14).

Then God is calling you to follow Him now. Will you be too busy or not interested in following Him? Where do you belong?

Day 61 - Prayer

Father God, I worship You for calling me to join Your family. It is so good to have You as my Father in Heaven. Let me tell others how good this is, so they will want to join Your family, too. I cannot stop telling You, "Thank You" for making me part of Your family. In Jesus' name. Amen.

Day 62 - Jesus' First Miracle

One day, Jesus and His disciples were invited to a wedding in Cana of Galilee. Jesus' mother, Mary, was also there. Everyone enjoyed themselves, eating and drinking merrily.

Then, Jesus' mother came to Him and said, "The wine is finished."

That was not a very good thing for the new husband and wife. People would say bad things about them when they found out there was no more wine. Mary wanted to help them. That was why she came to Jesus. She knew He could work miracles. Jesus decided to help them. So, He told the servants to fill six huge clay jars with water. Then He told them to draw some out of the jars and give them to the master of the feast. When the servants took what they drew out of the jars to the master of the feast, the water had turned into wine. The servants told everyone about it, which helped many people to believe that Jesus was indeed the Son of God.

That was the first miracle of Jesus.

Hallelujah!

Have you ever been to a wedding before?

Did you eat? What kind of food did you eat?

What kind of drink did you drink?

Day 63 - Prayer

My Most High God, thank You for Your Son, Jesus. He was so kind and good to these people. I know He wants to be like that to me, too. Let me always remember to come to You when I have a problem and to obey what You tell me to do. Thank You because You said You would answer me if only I would dare to ask You anything in the name of Jesus. I know; I have to ask according to Your Word, though. Thank You, my Promise Keeper. In your name, I pray. Amen.

Day 64 - Nicodemus Talks to Jesus

Jesus went around Judea and other places, telling people about the Kingdom of God and how to get into it. But not everyone understood what He was saying. Some of them who did not understand wanted to know more. One such man was Nicodemus. He was a ruler among the Jews. He taught them the Word of God. Even so, he did not understand what Jesus was talking about. So, he went and ask Him on his own.

He came to Jesus one night and talked with Him. Jesus told him many things about God's Kingdom and how to enter it. Nicodemus learned a lot from Jesus about the Kingdom that night. When we don't understand something, it is always a good thing for us to ask.

Jesus always preached about the Kingdom of God. What is the Kingdom of God, anyway?

What do you have to do to enter the Kingdom of God?

Day 65 - Prayer

Dear God, thank You for being so friendly to people. Lord, sometimes I want to talk to Jesus like Nicodemus did. I have so many questions I want to ask. Teach me to read Your Words every day so that I can find some answers. Thank You for helping me with Your Word. In Jesus' name. Amen.

Day 66 - Be Kind to One Another

One Sabbath day, Jesus was in a synagogue teaching the people. Sabbath was the day God told the Jews to rest and not work. Some of the Pharisees, the Jewish holy men, were there. There was also a man with a withered hand. They watched Jesus closely to see if Jesus was going to heal the man on the Sabbath day. Jesus then asked them if it was good to do good on the Sabbath day. He wanted to know if they would say He broke God's rule if He helped someone who was sick on a Sabbath day.

Jesus said, "Is it right to take your sheep out of a hole it fell on the Sabbath day?"

They all knew the sheep would die if no one took them out. So, the answer was yes. To show them that this was true, Jesus healed the withered hand of the man. No one could say anything. They now knew that saving someone's life or doing good to someone on the Sabbath day was not wrong.

It is never wrong to do something good for someone.

Have you done something good for someone today?

What are some of the good things you do for people?

Day 67 - Prayer

G od, I bless Your name for always giving us good gifts. Sometimes, though, we don't want something good to be done for others because we are just mean and selfish like these people. Let me be happy when You do good things for others. Lord, I thank You because Your bank of good stuff for us does not run out. In Jesus' name. Amen.

Day 68 - Jesus Helps a Woman from Samaria

J esus and His disciples were going to Jerusalem. To get there, Jesus went by the town of Samaria even when He knew that the Samaritans and the Jews were enemies. They hardly even talked to each other. Jesus and His disciples were all hungry and thirsty. So He sent them to buy food while He sat alone by the well and waited for them.

As He sat there, a woman from Samaria came to the well to get water, and Jesus asked her for some water to drink. She was surprised that Jesus spoke to her because she was a Samaritan, and the Jews did not talk to them. But Jesus spoke kindly to her and told her He was the promised Savior. She believed Him and ran to tell others about the good news. The other Samaritans quickly came, and Jesus taught them. They were so happy to have met Jesus, the promised Savior.

We must always be kind to others and share the good news about Jesus with people.

Will you be able to talk to someone who hates you as Jesus did?

What will you do if you talk to the person and he refuses to answer or speak to you roughly?

Day 69 - Prayer

Father, thank you for giving me the power to talk to people about You and Your wonders. Please help me tell others about You all the time. Sometimes, I want to, but the words won't come, or I am afraid. Let me remember You are always with me and that You have not given me the spirit of fear, but of power, love, and a sound mind. Thank You, for Your Word is powerful. In Jesus' name. Amen.

Day 70 - Jesus Heals a Nobleman's Son

One of the things Jesus did when He was on earth was miracles and healing the sick. This way, people knew He was the Son of God. Many people believed in God when they saw the miracles Jesus did, and Jesus obeyed His Father and worked many mighty works.

This was one of them. A nobleman had a son who was very sick. He came and asked Jesus to follow him home so He could heal his son, but Jesus worked a miracle instead. He did not go to the nobleman's house, and he just told him that his son would be better when he arrived home. The nobleman did not doubt what Jesus said, and he believed Jesus. He returned home to discover that his child had recovered from his illness. That is the power of God at work.

Hallelujah!

When you are sick, what do you do?

Have you ever asked pain to get out of your body in the name of Jesus?

Day 71 - Prayer

God, You are so good. Your Son, Jesus Christ, healed people—the rich, poor, soldiers, women, and children from their diseases. That shows that You and Jesus love all of us, which makes me feel so good. I am happy You are my God and Father. Thank You again for Your goodness in my life. In Jesus' name. Amen.

Day 72 - The Healing of the Man Beside the Pool

Here is another healing miracle that Jesus did. There was a man who had been sick for thirty-eight years. That's a long, long time. He could not walk, and he waited by the pool at Bethesda every day, hoping to get better. Many other sick people were there, too.

You see..., often, an angel came down and stirred up the water in the pool. The first sick person who entered the pool after the angel stirred the water was healed! For this poor man, getting into the pool first was impossible because someone always stepped in before him.

One day, Jesus came by. Out of all the sick people, He spoke to this man and asked him if he wanted to get better. The man complained instead of saying, 'Yes.' Jesus didn't mind his complaining. He told the man to take up his bed and walk. Immediately, the man took up his bed and walked. He was healed by believing and obeying Jesus.

That was good news for the man because he stood up and took his bed the moment Jesus told him. No more complaining, hey?

Come to think of it, why do people complain?

What is the difference between complaining and making a point?

Day 73 - Prayer

My Father in Heaven, thank You so much for all the many blessings You have for me. Let me learn to obey You so I can receive the blessings You have stored up for me. I know, for sure, that it must have been a very happy day for the sick man. I am so glad when You do great things for others and me. Dear Lord, there are lots of children in the hospital. Some are even in the Intensive Care Unit (ICU) right now. Please help them, just like You helped the man at the pool. Thank You for always being so helpful. In Jesus' name. Amen.

Day 74 - The Story of the Lost Sheep

Jesus liked to tell stories to teach the people about God and His Kingdom. Once, He told them the story of the lost sheep. A man had one hundred sheep.

"Baa! Baa! Baa!" They were everywhere.

The shepherd took very good care of his sheep. He led them out to the green grass every day so they could eat. He watched over them while they ate so no animal could harm them. He brought them back home in the evenings and locked them into their pen. This way, he kept them safe. He counted them when he took them out and when he brought them back home. But one day, he counted them in the evening, and one was missing. He was very worried about this one sheep. So, he left the ninety-nine and looked for the one lost sheep. He never came back until he found that little sheep. He was so excited to have found the one sheep that he called his friends together to tell them the good news.

What do you think about the shepherd? Was he greedy or caring? Why was he greedy or caring?

Day 75 - Prayer

I want to bless Your name, dear Lord, for always guiding us. Sometimes, God, I feel like a little lamb that runs away and does naughty things. Father God, Jesus is the Good Shepherd. Please help me be a good little lamb and obey everything He tells me to do. Thank You, Lord, for always keeping an eye out for me and bringing me back whenever I get away. In Jesus' name. Amen.

Day 76 - The Son Who Went Away

Jesus told a story about a man who had two sons. They lived with him and worked on his farm.

One day, the younger son said to his father, "Please, give me the money that is mine."

The father gave him the money that belonged to him. A few days later, the younger son packed his things and went away to a distant place to live. There, he partied, had fun, and spent all of his money. When he finished using all his money, his friends left him. He had nowhere to go and no food to eat. He had to find a job. The son ended up working on a pig farm. Sometimes, he was so hungry that he ate some of the pigs' food for dinner.

Yuck!

Life was very hard. He was unhappy, so he came to his senses and decided that he did not want to live like this. Then he remembered his father's house, where there was always food and many servants. Maybe he should return there. But what would his father say and do to him? Would he chase him away or take him back?

What do you do when you offend your parents or anyone?

What does it takes to say, "I'm sorry"?

Day 77 - The Boy Returns to His Home

The younger son kept wondering what his father would do to him as he traveled back home. He had left home a long time ago, and now he was coming back. But things were different now. He had gone with lots of money, and now he had none. He'd left with many fancy clothes; now, they were old, dirty, and torn up. Then, he had lots of food to eat, but now he was starving. He had spent all his money doing foolish things. He had been a very naughty boy, and now he felt very sorry for all the bad things he had done.

As he came closer to their house, he saw his father's house way down the road. Maybe he could turn back, or he should try to sneak inside without his father knowing right away. Yes, that would be a good thing for him to do. But as he came nearer, he saw someone running down the road towards him.

Oh no! It was his father!

What was he going to do now?

If you were this young man, what would you have done?

Day 78 - Prayer

I bless You, dear Lord, for Your mercies are new every morning. God, when I do wrong things and go away from You, please don't let me stay away forever. Let me feel sorry and come back to You because You are a good Father. Thank You for constantly receiving me whenever I come back. In Jesus' name. Amen.

Day 79 - The Kind Father

T he son stood up and watched his father running down the road towards him. He was too far away to see if his father was happy or mad. As his father came closer, the son looked at his face, and it was filled with joy as he rushed up to him, then his father hugged him tightly.

"Oh, my son! I'm so glad to see you!"

The younger son could not believe what he was hearing. His father was happy to have him back.

"Father, I am sorry for what I did," he said, sobbing. "I am not fit to be called your son. Let me be just a servant in your house."

But his father was not listening to him. He was calling his servants. "Bring the best robe, shoes, and my special ring for my son. Hurry and kill the best cow so we can have a feast."

The son could not believe the kindness of his father. He had forgiven him for all the wrong things he had done. It was the most beautiful thing that had ever happened to him.

Just like this father, God is ready to forgive us, too, for any wrong things we have done once we are truly sorry.

Was it right for the father to forgive his son after all he had done?

What does it mean to forgive someone?

Day 80 - Prayer

T hank You, Father God, for always being so forgiving. Help me remember that You always love me, no matter what I do. I can always come back to You and ask for Your forgiveness. Your arms, O Lord, are always wide open to receive and forgive me. That is wonderful to know. You are so awesome, God, and I love you so much! In Jesus' name. Amen.

Day 81 - The Older Brother

T he father was thrilled that his long-lost son had found his way home. He had a party for him. The food was cooking; the music was playing, and there was a lot of laughing and talking.

Now, this father also had an older son. He was well behaved and had stayed at home with his father. Like the younger son, he had never taken his things and left home. He was at work in the fields when his brother came back. As this older brother came near the house, he heard the music.

"What's going on?' he asked one of the servants.

"Oh, your brother has returned home, and your father is happy. He's having a party for him."

"A party, you say?' he asked, to make sure he was getting it right.

"Yes," replied the servant. "Isn't it great?"

What do you think the older brother is going to say to this?

Face it, if you were him, what would you have done?

Day 82 - Prayer

God, I want to thank You for Your Word that says the angels in Heaven are happy when we are born into Your family. They are so glad for even one person that receives you. They rejoice, sing, and shout, "Hallelujah, to the Lord! Someone has come home!" Thank You, Lord God, for loving us so much that You hold a party in Heaven for a saved soul. In Jesus' name. Amen.

Day 83 - The Angry Brother

The older brother could not believe what he was hearing. His younger brother had run off and did not tell them where he was. He had left him to do all the hard work, and now he has come back, and his father is giving him a party. Did their father forget that he took all the money and has come back home with none of it? His father must be crazy to be throwing a party for one who had acted up. Well, he will not attend the party. He was too angry and upset. He decided to stay outside until it was over. That was just not right. And he was going to let his father know how he felt about it.

What do you think happened after this?

What do you do when things don't go as planned?

Day 84 - Prayer

Father, thank You because You are always blessing people. Let me not be angry when You do good things for others. We all belong to You, and everything is Yours to give to whomever You wish. Let me be happy that You bless others, too. Thank You for Your many blessings. In Jesus' name. Amen.

Day 85 – What About Me?

The older brother was very angry with his father for throwing a party for his younger brother. So, he decided not to go to the party. He stayed outside, and his father came looking for him.

"Why aren't you inside at the party?" he asked.

"Because I don't think you are fair to me?" the older son said.

"What do you mean?" his father asked.

"Imagine, I have been here with you all the time. I did all the work while my brother was away, and you have never had a party for me."

"Oh, my son," his father said. "Don't you know that all I have is yours, and if you wanted a party, all you had to do was ask?"

"But...but...this son of yours wasted all that money, and you still welcome him back?" he said.

"Yes, son...he says he is sorry, and I have forgiven him...this is what fathers do because they love their children."

"I am a forgiving father...my love will not let me do anything else... and you must learn to forgive him, too."

The father was right. God tells us that we must always forgive those who have done wrong.

Has anyone done wrong to you?

Were you able to forgive the person?

Day 86 - Prayer

G od, I bless Your name for Your kindness. Help me not to be like this older brother. He did not want to forgive his younger brother. Let me obey Your Word, which says we are to forgive each other and be happy when God forgives others, no matter how naughty they have been. Thank You for always forgiving us. In Jesus' name. Amen.

Day 87 - A Roman Soldier Believes in Jesus

J esus was busy preaching and teaching the people. They came from all over to hear this new teacher. When he went to a town named Capernaum, a Roman soldier came to Him. Now the Romans were the rulers of the Jews, and they were not friends. Sometimes, the soldiers treated the Jews badly and even killed them. While He was in the town, the soldier came to Him. He asked Jesus to heal his servant, who was very sick.

Jesus said to the Roman soldier, "I will come to your house and heal him."

But the soldier said, "No, You don't have to come. You can just speak from here, and my servant will be healed."

Jesus was amazed at the man for believing so much in Him. So, He told him that he would find his servant well when he got back home.

It happened just as Jesus said, and the soldier was pleased.

What made you think the Roman soldier was able to believe so much in the Word that Jesus would speak?

Day 88 - Prayer

Dear God, thank You for You are love. Help me have the kind of faith that believes what You say right away. Your Word says if we do not have faith, we cannot please You. I want to please You all the time, so help me always believe and do what You tell me. Thank You because You have done everything from the very beginning. In Jesus' name. Amen.

Day 89 - Jesus Calms the Sea

One beautiful day, Jesus and His disciples were crossing over a sea on a ship. He was tired from talking to people all day. He fell asleep at the back of the boat. Suddenly, the winds started to blow, and a big storm came up. It rocked the ship up and down. The disciples were very afraid.

"We're all going to drown!" they cried.

Then one of them said, "But Jesus is on the ship. Let's ask Him to help us."

Quickly, they found Jesus and woke Him up.

"Master," they said. "Help us, or we're all going to die."

Very calmly, Jesus stood up and said to the sea, "Peace, be still."

At that moment, the winds stopped, and the waves calmed down. Jesus even had power over the sea! His disciples were amazed.

Do you know you have power in the words you speak?

Oh, yes! That is why you should mind what you say every time.

Day 90 - Prayer

I love You, Lord, because You are always with us. When I am afraid, God, please let me trust You. I believe I can face anything so long as You are with me. Let me remember Your promise never to leave me by myself or let me face any trouble alone. Remind me to always call upon You whenever I am afraid. Thank You, Lord, because You said You would answer us whenever we call on You. In Jesus' name. Amen.

Day 91 – The Wise Man and the Foolish Man

J esus told a story about two men. One of them was wise, and the other was foolish. Both men were building their houses. The wise man took a lot of time making his house. He wanted it to last. So, he dug deep into the rock to ensure it would not fall easily. The foolish man was in a hurry. He did not want to dig deep. That took too much time. So, he built his house on the sand.

The foolish man finished his house long before the wise man could finish his house. He might have been lying down and wondering what the wise man was doing for so long!

Then the heavy winds and rains came and beat upon the two houses. What do you think happened? Right. The wise man's house did not fall, but the foolish man's house crashed. So be smart and make sure you build your life on Jesus, the Solid Rock, and the Chief Corner Stone.

Have you ever built a sandcastle on the beach before?

Have you built a tent either during camping or make-believe?

What did you use to build them?

Did they stand when the wind blew?

Day 92 - Prayer

T hank You because You are a gracious God. My Father, I always want to be wise and do things the way You say I should. Let me not be foolish like this man and lose everything because I did not build my life on Your Word. I want my house to be standing after the storms of life are over. Thank You for making me wise. In Jesus' name. Amen.

Day 93 - The Many Seeds

J esus again told a story about a farmer who went out into the field to sow seeds. He took a handful out of the bag and scattered them about. Some seeds fell by the wayside. The hungry birds quickly came and ate them up. That was the end of those seeds. They did not have time to grow. The next set of seeds fell on stones and not into the ground. A bit of soil was there, so they grew up quickly. But the sun's heat dried them up, and they died. The third set of seeds fell among thorns and weeds. They grew for a while. But then, many thorns and weeds grew up around them and choked them. So, they, too, died. Oh-oh! Poor farmer, he only has one set of seeds left now. What is going to happen to those seeds? The last set of seeds fell upon the farmer's good ground prepared for them. And guess what? They grew and bore many other seeds.

The wayside, stones, thorns/weeds, and finally, the good ground, represent the different hearts of people. Which ground do you think Jesus would want your heart to be like? Why did you choose your answer?

Day 94 - Prayer

I thank You, Lord, for always being so good. Lord God, give me a heart like the good ground, so my life will show how good You are. Let me not be in too much of a hurry to grow or be so busy doing what I want that I have no time to serve You. Help me make obeying Your Word the most important thing in my life. Thank You for everything You have done for me. In Jesus' name. Amen.

Day 95 - The Wheat and the Tares

Jesus talked a lot about farming in His stories. He said God's Kingdom is like a farmer sowing seeds in his field. These are seeds that will bear other seeds, good for eating. But then, along comes an evil man who planted weeds in his field. He does this at night when no one is around. So, the farmer does not know that he is doing this. The wheat and the weeds grew together. Only when the seeds were growing and bearing fruit did the servants see the weeds. They hurried to the farmer and asked him if they should pull out the weeds now. But the farmer said no. They were to leave them to grow together until harvest time. Then he would separate the wheat from the weeds. The wheat he would use to make bread. Then, he would burn up the weeds because they were not good.

Have you ever seen a wheat farm before? If you have, what do they look when they are small and what do they look like when it is time for harvest?

Will you be wheat or weed seed? How?

Day 96 - Prayer

Lord, thank You for the power of choice You have given us—we can decide what we want to do. Dear Lord, I have decided to be like the wheat. I don't want to be a weed that looks good but is not. You know everything about us, God, for we cannot hide from You. When Jesus comes back to earth, everybody will know who was good and who was not. I want to be good right now and until You come. Please help me accomplish what I have decided on—being good all the time. Thank You for answering my prayers. In Jesus' name. Amen.

Day 97 - When Small Is Great

J esus liked to talk about seeds. They helped His listeners understand how the Kingdom of God worked. He told them about a mustard seed. It was one of the smallest seeds the people knew. Jesus said it was a very tiny seed, but it became a massive plant when it grew up. It was so big that birds of the air came and perched in it.

Think of that—something small can grow enormous for others to use. How about you? You are small, but God can use you in a big way in people's lives around you.

Are you willing to be used by God?

Name three ways you think God can use you to help others.

Day 98 - Prayer

God, I worship You because I am not too small to do something for You. Please tell me what You want me to do, and I will do it. I know I will not always be small. One day, I will grow up big. Then, I can do lots more things for You. Thank You for that. In Jesus' name. Amen.

Day 99 – Jesus Not Accepted in His Hometown

J esus was going around everywhere preaching, teaching, and healing people. Large crowds followed Him wherever He went. Then one day, He came back to Nazareth, where He grew up. Do you think the people were happy to see Him?

They were not.

They started to talk about how they knew Him from when He was a child. His brothers and sisters had grown up with them. His father, Joseph, was only a carpenter, and they knew His mother, Mary, very well. So, they decided Jesus was pretending to be somebody important when He wasn't.

However, they were wrong because Jesus was and is the Son of God and the Savior of the World. We all need Him because He is the most important person who has ever lived.

Never forget this!

Have you ever been rejected by a group of friends before?

If you have, how did you feel?

If you haven't, would you see it kind enough to pray for some people who want others to accept them, but they are not because maybe they are sick or something else?

Day 100 - Prayer

Father God, I praise You for being very good to me. My God, I want You to know that Jesus is always welcome where I am. I think He is so awesome and special. He left the beautiful Heaven and came to earth to live as a man. He went about teaching and doing good. That's real love! He did nothing wrong, and He paid the price for our sins by dying on the cross. You know what? Dear Lord, every time I think about Jesus leaving Heaven and everything He suffered for my sake, I always say, "Wow!" Thank You, Jesus, for being You. In Jesus' name. Amen.

Day 101 – The Little Boy's Lunch

One day, Jesus was preaching to many people in a desert place. They had been listening to Him all day. They had taken no food with them, and now they were all hungry. Jesus' disciples came and told Him to send the people away to get their food.

But Jesus said, "They do not have to go away. Give them something to eat."

The disciples looked at Him strangely and said, "All we have is a little boy's five loaves and two fishes. That was his lunch," they concluded.

Jesus said to His disciples, "Bring them to me."

He told His disciples to make the people sit down on the grass. Then He prayed and broke the five loaves and two fishes and gave them to His disciples to give to the people. They could not believe it. Every time they broke the bread and the fishes, there was always more left. Five thousand men, many women, and children ate from the fishes and the loaves that day.

That was a miracle.

Jesus is a great miracle worker.

What is a miracle? Are miracles still happening or not?

Day 102 - Prayer

God, thank You for always giving to people in need. Lord, this little boy was very kind. I want to be like Him and not be selfish. I want to give all I have to Jesus so He can use it to help others. Help me look around for people who need help and do what I can to help them—maybe give a drink of water or say sorry to someone crying. Thank You because I know You will help me do this. In Jesus' name. Amen.

Day 103 – Peter Walks on Water

Peter and some of Jesus' disciples were in a boat on the sea. The winds were blowing strongly, and the waves were very high. The disciples were terrified, especially since Jesus was not with them. Then suddenly, they saw someone coming toward them. It must be a ghost because people can't walk on water. Now they were terrified. Then, as the person came nearer, they realized it was Jesus. But they were still not sure.

So, Peter said, "Jesus, if that is You, let me come to You on the water."

Jesus told him, "Come."

Then Peter stepped out of the boat. And guess what? He walked on top of the water. Peter could not believe it! He was doing the impossible. Yes, with Jesus' help, we can do the impossible, too.

How would you feel if you saw someone walking on top of the water on the beach?

Day 104 - Prayer

Miracle Worker, I bow before You today. God, this was a very wondrous miracle. I want to walk on water, too. That must be very cool! That tells me again that we can do all things with Your help. For now, while I might not walk on water, please help me trust You to do whatever You tell me. I now know that whatever You ask us to do, we can do it with Your help. Thank You because You said we should ask, and whatever we ask in the name of Jesus, we will receive it. In Jesus' name. Amen.

Day 105 - The Forgiving Master

Once again, Jesus told a story. He said there was a servant of a rich man. He borrowed lots of money from his master, and the servant could not pay it back. His master decided to sell him and his family to pay for the money he owed, but the servant fell at the feet of his master and begged him to have mercy on him. The master forgave him. The servant did not have to pay back the money, and his master did not sell him and his family.

Now, this same servant had a friend who had borrowed money from him, and the friend could not pay him back.

What do you think this servant did to his friend?

Day 106 - Prayer

T hank You, our Most High God, for being so kind to forgive us when we do wrong. Thank You because You have forgiven me for all my sins. Thank You for preparing a place in Heaven where I will live with You forever one day. I bless Your name, O God. In Jesus' name. Amen.

Day 107 - The Unforgiving Servant

D o you remember the servant whose master had for-given the money he owed him? He was very, very glad about it. This same man had a friend who owed him lesser money and could not pay him back. He became very upset with his friend and threw him into prison. When the other servants heard about it, they thought it was a terrible thing to do. They knew how their master had forgiven him for his debt. So why could he not do the same for his friend? These servants went and told their master what this servant had done. His master was upset and threw the unforgiving servant into prison. He was happy to be forgiven for the money he owed, but he did not want to forgive his friend.

We must always learn to treat others how we want them to treat us.

Come to think of it, is it easy to forgive someone?

Whatever your answer is, you can do everything through Christ that gives you strength.

Day 108 - Prayer

Dear God in Heaven, thank You so much for forgiving me of my sins even before I was born. I know I do not always treat others how I want them to treat me, and I think more about what I want and how I will receive it. Let me remember that You know my thoughts, whether good or bad. Please help me put myself in the place of others when I am talking or playing with them. Thank You for being so kind to us. In Jesus' name. Amen.

Day 109 - Who Is My Neighbor?

"Love your neighbor as yourself," says the Bible.

A particular lawyer heard this and wanted Jesus to tell him who was the neighbor he was supposed to love. Most people think your neighbor is someone who lives near you. Jesus told the lawyer this story to show him and us who our neighbor is.

One day, a Jew was going from Jerusalem to Jericho. Some thieves attacked and robbed him. They wounded him and left him to die. A certain priest (a Jew) came by, and when he saw the wounded man, he walked to the other side of the road and went away. A Levite (also a Jew) came along. He, too, looked at the bleeding man and did the same thing as the priest. Poor man, nobody wanted to help him. He was certainly going to die. Then a Samaritan came along. When he saw the man, he looked at him. He saw he was hurt.

And what do you think he did?

Day 110 - Prayer

My Father and God, thank You for loving me so much, even if I don't realize it. You said we are to love our neighbor as we love ourselves. Sometimes, I, too, wonder who my neighbor is. I can't wait to hear the following story to find out. I am so excited! Thank You, Jesus, for being my best storyteller. In Jesus' name. Amen.

Day 111 - The Good Neighbor

The man from Samaria looked at the man lying in the pool of blood at the side of the road. He was left there, hurt and bleeding, by the robbers. What was the Samaritan going to do? Would he walk away like the other two men? He felt sorry for the man, so he stopped and helped him. He did not know him, but this did not matter. He saw he needed help. So, he tied up his cuts after pouring oil and wine on them. Then the Samaritan traveler put the injured man on his donkey and took him to an inn. There, he paid the innkeeper to take care of him. He also promised to stop by and check on him the next time he came by.

Which of the three individuals do you think was a good neighbor to this man? If your answer is the Samaritan, then you are right. The good neighbor was the Samaritan, who stopped to help the wounded man. Now, you know our neighbor is anyone needing our help. We do not need to know them, and they don't have to be our friends.

We are here to help each other.

Have you helped someone you didn't know before?

What kind of expression did you see on their face?

Day 112 - Prayer

Father God, thank You for helping me know who my neighbor is. I want to be a good neighbor. Let me stop and help other children at my school, even if they are not my friends or I don't know them. I know now that my neighbor does not have to live next to me or be my friend. Help me be kinder and more caring to those who need help. Thank You, O God, for giving us, good neighbors. In Jesus' name. Amen.

Day 113 - Zacchaeus wants to See Jesus

Zacchaeus was a very short man. He was so short that other people looked like giants to him. However, he was an important man and very rich. One day, Zacchaeus heard Jesus was coming to his town for a visit. He had heard about all the wonderful things Jesus was doing. Zacchaeus wanted to see Him. But wherever Jesus went, large crowds followed Him. Zacchaeus knew he would not stand a chance of seeing Jesus in the crowd because he was so short. Aha! He was going to climb up in a tree right where Jesus was going to pass. This way, he could look down and see Him.

Do you think Zacchaeus' plan worked?

Day 114 - Prayer

Lord God, I worship You because You know our heart, and You will always show yourself to anyone that wants to see You. Sometimes, God, I feel like Zacchaeus. I don't fit in with the others, and they tease me. Help me not let that keep me from coming to You because You know all about me and love me the way I am. I want to see You one day, so I will keep following You. Thank You because I know You will always show Yourself to me even when problems and difficulties are trying to keep me from seeing You. In Jesus' name. Amen.

Day 115 - Zacchaeus Meets Jesus Part 1

Zacchaeus wanted to see Jesus very much. But he was very short. So, he looked for a tree that hung right over the road where Jesus was going to walk. As Jesus came along the road, He saw the crowds and heard the loud chatter of the people. Long before He and the crowds came, Zacchaeus climbed up into the sycamore tree and hid. Everyone was excited. Zacchaeus could hardly wait as Jesus got closer to the tree. He would be right over Jesus' head, and no one would see him. He watched as Jesus came along the road. Then, as He came under the sycamore tree, He stopped right below Zacchaeus. Zacchaeus watched to see what He was going to do. Then Jesus looked up into the tree, exactly where Zacchaeus was hiding.

He said, "Zacchaeus, hurry and come down. For today, I must go with you to your house."

How do you think Zacchaeus felt? And what did he do?

Day 116 - Zacchaeus Meets Jesus Part 2

J esus came and stood right under the tree where Zacchaeus was hiding. Then He called Zacchaeus by his name and told him to come down from the tree. How did Jesus know Zacchaeus was up in the tree?

Zacchaeus was amazed that Jesus knew his name and where he was hiding. Jesus knew because He is the Son of God, and like His Father, God, He knows everything. Zacchaeus was so happy to have Jesus come to his house, which was much better than just seeing Him. He hurried down the tree and took Jesus home with him.

Would you be happy if Jesus came to your house today?

What would you show and tell Him?

Day 117 - Prayer

Father God, thank You for always showing Yourself to us. God, Jesus knew all about Zacchaeus, and He even knew his name and where he was hiding in the tree. Wow! I am glad that You know all about me and want me to be a part of Your family, which makes me so happy. Thank You, my Father, for inviting me into Your family. In Jesus' name. Amen.

Day 118 – Jesus Goes Home with Zacchaeus

O f course, Zacchaeus must have given Jesus something to eat, and since other people came along, they must have had some food.

As Jesus talked with Zacchaeus, the little man said, "Jesus, I am going to give half of all I own to the poor."

Jesus must have been very excited to hear this. I am sure the poor people were glad to hear this, too, for Zacchaeus was a wealthy man.

Then Zacchaeus said, "And all those people I have cheated to become rich, I will give them back four times what I took from them."

Now Zacchaeus must have sounded like a madman to be doing these things.

Why would he want to do this?

When Jesus comes to visit us, we want to be kind and good, just like Him. That was what happened with Zacchaeus. The joy of seeing Jesus, knowing that Jesus knew him, and accepted him, even if he was a fraud, made him want to do good things to show Jesus that he was grateful.

What good deed do you want to accomplish today for Jesus?

Day 119 - Prayer

Lord Jesus, thank You so much for being a friend of sinners. Father God, I would be so happy if Jesus came to my house today because there are many things I want to tell, show, and ask Him. But since I can't see You with my physical eyes but see You with my heart, I will keep talking to You when I pray. Thank You for making a way for me to speak to You whenever I want. In Jesus' name. Amen.

Day 120 - The Rich Young Ruler

O nce there was a wealthy young man. He went to the temple to pray. He read his Bible, and he tried to be kind to everyone. One day, he came to hear Jesus teach.

He asked Jesus, "What must I do to live forever?"

Jesus told him he had to keep all of God's commandments. The young man told Jesus that he had kept them all since childhood, and that sounded very good.

Then Jesus told him, "Okay, then sell everything you have, then come and follow Me."

Did the young man do this?

No, because he was wealthy and loved his money more than God. We must be cautious so that loving money or anything else does not keep us from following or obeying God.

What is your best game?

Do you get angry when your parents ask you to stop playing your game so you can do your chores?

Day 121 - Prayer

T hank You, Lord, for Your teachings are true. God, help me not love money or anything else better than You. Jesus said it is tough for a rich man to enter God's Kingdom, and it is true. When we have lots of things, we might forget about You and trust in the things we have instead. Thank You for always being there to help us. In Jesus' name. Amen.

Day 122 - The Foolish Rich Man

There was once a farmer who had lots of lands. He planted much grain, and the ground bore a lot of wheat. That made him very happy.

He said to himself, 'What will I do with all this wheat?'

Then he had an excellent idea. He would pull down all his old barns and build bigger ones. This way, he could store up all his wheat. He would have a lot of food to enjoy for a very long time. He was only thinking about himself, and he did not think of giving any to the poor people, who had no farms or wheat. He didn't even recognize God, who had made him wealthy.

That night, God said to him, "You are foolish because tonight you will die and who will get all your wheat?"

It must have shocked the man to hear this. God wanted him to know that it was not good to think only of yourself and not of others. When God blesses you with a lot, you are to give some to those who do not have as much as you.

Have you ever given something to someone who has not?

How did you feel doing that good deed?

Day 123 - Prayer

Father God, I praise You, for You are the giver of life. Help me be kind with the things You have given me. You like it when we share what we have with others, because this is what You have done for us. You share Your love and Your goodness with us every day. You give us rain, sunshine, food, and many other things. But more than anything else, you gave Your Son, the Lord Jesus Christ, to us. Thank You for such a wonderful gift! In Jesus' name. Amen.

Day 124 - The Proud Pharisee

A Pharisee was a very religious man in Jesus' day. He studied the Bible, and he was always praying. There was one proud Pharisee who thought he did everything right. Then there was the Publican, a man who knew little about the Bible. He did not pray and knew he did wrong things.

One day, the two went up to the temple to pray. The Pharisee looked at the Publican. Then he said to God, "Thank You I am not like this man. I fast, pray, and give money to You. I am sure this Publican does not do as much as I."

The publican knew he was not always good. So, he asked God to forgive him for the bad things he had done.

Jesus told the people that God accepted the Publican's prayer. He was unhappy with the Pharisee's prayer because he was proud and thought he was better. God hates pride, and He prefers when we are humble, like the Publican.

Which one sounds like you?

Day 125 - Prayer

God, I bless Your holy name for who You are. Help me not to be proud like the Pharisee. Your Word tells us that You hate pride. We also know that it goes before a fall. You also tell us that You will fight against those who are proud. When we are proud, we only think about ourselves and not others. That is not good. Please give me a meek and humble spirit that will not boast and think that I am better than other people. Thank You for the answer. In Jesus' name. Amen.

Day 126 - Too Busy For God

Once a king's son was going to get married. He invited all his family and friends to the wedding. The king prepared a large feast when the day came and waited for his guests to arrive. But many of them did not show up. They gave him all kinds of excuses for why they could not attend. Some had gone to their farms, and another to look at something new he had bought. They were just too busy doing their own thing. The king was very upset. So, he sent his servants into town to invite anyone who wanted to come. Many people came and enjoyed the feast that the others had missed.

Sometimes, we are too busy for God, and we miss the blessings He wants us to have.

What always keeps you busy?

Day 127 - Prayer

Dear God, thank You because You are not too busy for us. May I never be too busy for You, O Lord. Let me find time to talk with You, read Your Word, pray and worship You. Help me put You first in my life. Thank You, wonderful God. In Jesus' name. Amen.

Day 128 – The Ten Lepers

As Jesus was going through a particular village, He met ten lepers. These were people with terrible skin diseases. Because other people could catch it from them, they had to live by themselves. No family or friends could come near them. Imagine how they felt. They cried out to Jesus from afar and begged Him to heal them. Jesus told the ten lepers to go and show themselves to the priest. As they obeyed Him and went, they received their healing. Can you imagine how happy they were? But only one of the ten ran back to Jesus and gave Him thanks.

We must never forget to thank God for the good things He does for us every day.

Do you remember to thank God when you wake up every morning?

Do you thank your parents before you eat or after you have eaten?

Day 129 - Prayer

L et us give thanks to our God, for He is good. Let us praise Him for the good works He has done for all of us. He sends rain on the good and the bad. He gives us life, health, and strength. Let us praise Him for all the blessings He gives us. Let us thank Him for His mercy and forgiveness. Let everyone thank and praise the Lord. Hallelujah! In Jesus' name. Amen.

Day 130 – The Ten Bridesmaids

J esus told a story about a young woman who was getting married. She asked ten of her friends to be her brides-maids. They got dressed and were waiting to be taken to the wedding. They waited all day until night came. They were tired and fell asleep. Then they heard the bridegroom had arrived in the middle of the night. It was time to get to the wedding. They quickly woke up, put on their clothes, and grabbed their lamps. They needed the light from the lamp to get to the wedding because it was dark. But only five of them had oil in their lamps. The other five did not. So only those who had the oil went off to the wedding. They left the other five behind and they missed the wedding.

That tells us we will miss out on essential things if we are not ready.

You or your parents, who get ready for a church service first?

Have you ever missed a great function because you were not ready in time?

Do you like waiting for people?

Do you go to school late? Why?

Day 131 - Prayer

God, thank You for giving us a Promised Land—Heaven. I want to be ready when You come back to earth to take us there. Let me do everything as Your Word tells me. I want to keep shining for You until You come. Heavenly Father, help me be ready when Jesus comes back for us. I mean this prayer with all my heart. You have always answered me when I ask You for something. Thank You for that. In Jesus' name, I pray. Amen.

Day 132 – Jesus Rides on a Donkey

O n the last week of Jesus' life on earth, He wanted His people, the Jews, to know that He was the King God had promised them long ago. So, He sent His disciples to get a donkey for Him to ride on. He especially wanted to ride on a donkey. You see...; it was already written in the Bible that their King would one day come to them, riding on a donkey. Jesus knew that this was the day for Him to do that. He told His disciples where to find the donkey and that they should tell the owner He needed to use it. The disciples saw the donkey, as Jesus said, and the owner gave it to them. When they came back, they put some of their clothes on the donkey for Jesus to sit on. Then they set off for Jerusalem.

What kind of vehicle does your president, prime minister, king, or ruler use when going to a function?

Does your ruler have a driver and escort personnel?

What example do you think Jesus showed us when He rode on a donkey?

Day 133 - Prayer

Father, thank You because Jesus has shown me an excellent example of being humble. Jesus was so humble that He rode on a donkey. Let me not be proud and boastful or try to show off. I want to be just like Jesus. Lord, I praise Your name because I know You will help me deal with pride. In Jesus' name. Amen.

Day 134 - Jesus Goes to Jerusalem

J esus rode on a donkey to Jerusalem. His disciples followed Him. As He got near the city, the people came out to meet Him. Some remembered that the Bible said their King would come to them riding on a donkey. They believed Jesus was from the family of King David.

So, they started shouting, "Hosanna to the Son of David! Blessed is He who comes in the name of the Lord!"

The disciples were also shouting praises to God for all the miracles and good things Jesus had been doing. People waved palm branches and spread them on the ground with their garments for the donkey to walk on, creating a lot of noise. They welcomed Jesus like a king. Oh, of course, Jesus is the King of Kings.

If Jesus showed up in your town, what would you do? And did the leaders of the Jews crown Jesus as a king?

Day 135 - Prayer

Father God, I worship Your name because of the gift of Your Son to us. I welcome Your Son, Jesus Christ, as King into my heart. He is a wonderful, kind, and loving King. I bow down and worship Him today for what He did for us all. Please help me tell others about Him so that they will come and worship Him. Thank You, Jesus, for always being willing to enter the heart of anyone that wants You in their life. In Jesus' name. Amen.

Day 136 - Jesus and the Leaders of the Jews

W hen Jesus, His disciples, and the people came into the city, everyone wondered what was happening. Why were the people so excited, crowding around Jesus and shouting, "Hosanna to the Son of David!' Blessed is He who comes in the name of the Lord!' Hosanna in the highest!" (Mathew 21:9).

"Who is this man?" the leaders asked the people because they did not believe Jesus was anyone special.

The people said, "Jesus, the prophet from Nazareth."

Some leaders told Jesus to tell His followers to be quiet and stop saying all those things about Him. But Jesus told them, "If the people did not speak, then the rocks would cry out."

That was Jesus' way of telling them that what the people were saying about Him was true. But the leaders did not want to believe it. For most of the week, Jesus taught the people in the temple in Jerusalem. But the leaders were very upset and kept thinking of a way to get rid of Him.

How would you feel if you tell someone who you are and the person does not believe thinking you are lying?

Since not everybody would believe what you say, what strategies do you need to learn to deal with such situations?

Day 137 - Prayer

Father, I worship You for being so generous in sending Your Son to save us. I know Jesus is unique. He is Your only Son, who came down from Heaven to save us from our sins, and He did it out of His great love for us. Thank You for sending Jesus. Jesus, thank You for coming to save us. In Jesus' name. Amen.

Day 138 - Martha and Mary

Jesus had some friends in Bethany. They were Martha, Mary, and their brother, Lazarus. He stayed at their house sometimes when He came to Jerusalem. Martha loved to cook, and whenever Jesus came, she busied herself in the kitchen. On one of His visits, she was very busy getting a meal ready. She was in the kitchen, but her sister, Mary, was sitting at Jesus' feet, listening to what He was saying. Martha got upset because Mary was not helping her. She went and complained to Jesus. Then Jesus told her that Mary had chosen to listen to Him, which was the better thing to do. She, Martha, was spending too much time in the kitchen. He told her she needed to spend more time with Him than cooking.

Just like Mary, we all need to spend more time with Jesus.

Name some ways we can spend time with Jesus.

What do you do with your parents when they spend time with you?

Day 139 – Prayer

God, thank You for putting Your Word in written form so we can use it to correct one another, as Jesus corrected Martha. Martha, Mary's sister, was too busy to listen to Jesus. That happens to me, too. I get busy with so many things that I do not have enough time to read my Bible and pray. Please help me know that talking and listening to You is the most crucial thing in my day. Please help me make more time to do this. Thank You, Lord, for everyone You are using to point me in the right direction. In Jesus' name. I pray. Amen.

Day 140 - Lazarus Gets Sick

One day, Lazarus, Jesus' friend, got sick. Jesus was far away, so Mary and Martha sent messengers to tell him about Lazarus. Mary and Martha were very upset and wondered why Jesus was not coming so He could heal their brother. They knew He could make Lazarus better. They waited and waited, but Jesus did not come. And so, their brother, Lazarus, died. Jesus reached their house four days after they had buried Lazarus. Mary and Martha wept and told Him their brother would not have died if He had come sooner.

Jesus told them not to worry, just to believe in Him, and they would see their brother again. They did not know how this would help now that they had buried their brother for four days. Then Jesus asked them to take Him to where they buried Lazarus.

What was Jesus going to do there?

Day 141 - Jesus Calls Lazarus From the Tomb

Mary and Martha wondered what Jesus was going to do at the tomb of Lazarus, their brother. He was already dead and buried for four days. But they obeyed Jesus and took Him to the grave. When Jesus arrived there, He, too, cried because Lazarus was His friend. They buried Lazarus in a cave with a big stone covering its mouth, and Jesus told them to take away the stone. They wondered if Jesus knew what He was doing, but they did as He asked, regardless.

Then Jesus prayed and said in a loud voice, "Lazarus, come forth!"

Everyone waited to see what would happen.

Have you ever spoken to anything that cannot reply to you before?

What did you speak to?

Day 142 - Prayer

Thank You, God, for Your assurance of hope for everyone that believes in Your Son, Jesus Christ. Jesus says He will bring us back to life one day, even if we die now. That is very hard to understand, but I believe it is true. Lord, I can't wait to see that wonderful day. Thank You for it.

Father God, thank You because You can do all things. Help me accept that You may not answer our prayers right away. Please help me trust that You know what is best for me. I bless Your name for doing everything for my good. In Jesus' name. Amen.

Day 143 - Lazarus Comes Alive Again

M ary, Martha, Jesus' disciples, and other people waited to see what would happen. Jesus had gone to Lazarus' tomb and called for him to come out of it. Nobody on earth had ever done anything like this before. They were surprised to see Lazarus sit up in the tomb as they waited, and he was still wrapped up in the pieces of cloth they had buried him in.

Jesus said, "Lose him and let him go!"

Some braver persons, who were not trembling in fear and awe, ran towards Lazarus and unwrapped him. He was happy to be alive again, and so were his two sisters.

Everyone could not stop talking about the incredible power that Jesus had. As the Son of God, He can bring people back from the dead.

That is awesome!

Jesus had that great power, and He gave it to you, too, so you can use it whenever you need to. Now you can speak to pain to get out of your body, and you can speak smartness, grace, etc., into your life. Please speak nothing negative concerning you or other people.

What are you going to speak to today?

Day 144 - Prayer

God, thank You for Your power of resurrection. It was an amazing miracle for Jesus to bring back Lazarus from the dead. That tells me He is Your beloved Son, who can do anything. I know we will all die someday, but because of what He said and did when raising Lazarus, I know that one day, He will bring all God's children back to live with Him forever. I can hardly wait for that lovely day to come. Even so, hurry, and come back, Lord Jesus. Thank You again for that great day. In Jesus' name. Amen.

Day 145 - The Ten Talents

This is a story Jesus told of a rich man who had many servants. The rich man was going away on a long trip. So, he called his servants together. He gave them some money, called talents, to look after while he was away. He gave one ten, the other five, and one to the third person. He told them to use the money he had given them wisely to make more money for him.

They call that investing so that the money you have will become more. After being away for a very long time, the master came back. He called his three servants to see what they had done with his money.

What do you think they all did with the money he gave them?

Day 146 - Prayer

God, thank you for being so generous to me. I want to know what You have given me to use for You until Jesus comes back. I can do some things very well like dance, sing, play a sport, learn something and much more. Please, Lord, help me understand what You want me to do. Thank You for giving me so many talents. In Jesus' name. Amen.

Day 147 - The Wise Servants and the Foolish One

T he master called his servants to ask them about the money he had given them to use for him while he was away. The first servant used his ten talents and earned ten more. He now had twenty talents to give his master. The master was very pleased, and he made him ruler over ten cities. The other servant made five extra talents on his master's money. He had ten talents to give to his master. Again, the master praised him and asked him to rule over five cities. Then came the last servant, who had been given one talent. He gave back the one talent to his master. He told him he was afraid to do anything with it, so he had hidden it. The master was very upset with him for not doing anything with the money. So, he took it from him and gave it to the servant who had earned ten talents.

Jesus wanted his hearers to know that we must always use the talents God gives us, or we will lose them.

What would you use it for if you were given money to invest?

Day 148 - Prayer

God, I praise You because You created every one of us, each filled with different talents. You promise to give us prizes for the work we do for You while we live on earth. You have given all of us talents to use for You. Help me find my talent and use it well so that when You come back, You will say to me, "Well done!" Thank You for You are the Great Giver. In Jesus' name. Amen.

Day 149 - To Obey or Not to Obey

A certain man had two sons.

One day, he said to one of them, "Go and work on the farm today."

The son said, "Yes," but he did not go.

He said to his other son, "Go work on the farm today."

He said, "No."

But later, the one that said no changed his mind and went while the other son that said yes did not go. Jesus asked the people to tell Him which of the two sons was the obedient one. Was it the one who said he would go and did not? Or was it the one who said he would not go but, in the end, went?

I think you know which one it is—the second one. It is better to say no, and then do it than to say you're going to do it and don't. God wants us always to keep our promises.

Have you behaved like these two sons before?

When you said yes, why did you not keep to your promise?

When you said no, what changed your mind?

Day 150 - Prayer

L ord, thank You for promising to send Your son Jesus back to earth for all who believe. Help me keep my promise and do whatever You tell me to do. Let me not be too ready to say yes and then don't. Thank You for showing us several times that You will always keep Your promises to us, no matter what. In Jesus' name. Amen.

Day 151 - Dorcas, the Kind Woman

There was a woman named Dorcas living in Joppa. She heard the good news about Jesus Christ and became a Christian. Dorcas looked around her for something she could do to help others. She saw that many poor people did not have clothes. So, she made clothes for them. One day, she became sick and died. The people were crying, saying, "Dorcas was so good to us, and now she is gone. Who is going to sew clothes for us and help us?" Then they heard that Peter was preaching in a town nearby.

Quickly, they sent for him. They told him all about Dorcas' good works, and now she was dead. Peter went into the room, prayed to God, and told Dorcas to come back alive. God answered Peter's prayer, and the dead Dorcas came back to life. That is how we know Jesus has given His miracle-working power to His disciples.

Have you ever prayed for someone sick before? Oh..., don't say you are too little because God uses the rich, poor, elder, and little children.

Day 152 - Prayer

My faithful Father, thank You for the gift of feeling that You have given to us. Your Word tells us we should be kind to each other. I get a nice feeling when people are kind to me. Teach me how to be kind and help others. Help me follow Your example of kindness. Thank You, dear Lord. In Jesus' name. Amen.

Day 153 - Saul, the Enemy of Christians

S aul did not like the Christians at all. He didn't believe Jesus was God's Son. Because of this, after Jesus went back to Heaven, Saul tried to stop His disciples from telling people about Him. The priests in charge of Jerusalem's temple also thought the same way. So, Saul took letters from them to hunt down the Christians. When he found them, he was to bring them to Jerusalem to be tried and punished for believing in Jesus. You can imagine that every Christian was afraid of Saul and kept running away from him. That continued until something strange happened to Saul.

What would you do if someone asked you to stop talking about Jesus?

Day 154 - Prayer

God, thank You because You know everything about everyone. Sometimes people are unkind to me because I say I am a Christian, and they laugh at me and tease me. Help me be brave and not stop believing in You because of what they do or say. And for the unkind people who do not believe in You worldwide, please help Your children talk to them about You. Thank You for the answered prayers. In Jesus' name. Amen.

Day 155 - Paul Falls off His Horse

S aul started going to Damascus so he could hunt down the believers of Jesus Christ, and he would take them back to Jerusalem to be punished by the High Priest. Neither he nor the priests believed that Jesus Christ was the Son of God and the Savior of the World. They did not want Jesus' disciples telling this to other people.

Saul was riding on his horse with many soldiers. Suddenly, a light, brighter than the sun, appeared in the sky. It frightened Saul's horse, and he fell off. Then Saul heard a voice calling his name.

"Saul, Saul, why are you persecuting me?"

Immediately, Saul knew it was Jesus talking to him, and so he said, "Who are You, Lord?"

The voice said, "I am Jesus, who you are trying to hurt."

Saul knew what this meant. When you try to hurt God's people, it is like you are hurting God. We must never forget this.

What happened next?

Day 156 - Prayer

Dear God, I can't stop thanking You for Your Son, Jesus; who knows when someone is hurt. Let me remember that when I am hurting, You are there with me. It is like You, God, are hurting, too, because You live in my heart. Let me remember this and pray to You no matter how I feel. I praise You, O God, for always being with me. In Jesus' name. Amen.

Day 157 - Saul Becomes Blind

S aul and some soldiers were traveling to Damascus to find and lock up Christians. But as he was on the way, a bright light from Heaven shone around him, and he fell off his horse. Then he heard the voice of Jesus talking to him. Jesus told Saul to go into the city, and someone would come and tell him what to do. After hearing this and getting up from the ground, Saul realized he was blind. He could not see. The bright light from Heaven had hurt his eyes. Someone had to lead him around. They took him to a house in the city, and they left him there.

What was going to happen to Saul now?

Day 158 – Ananias Told to Visit Saul

Living in the city of Damascus was a man named Ananias. As a follower of Jesus Christ, he belonged to the group of people Saul was trying to lock up. One day, he was praying, and God spoke to him. He told him to go and visit Saul, who was staying in a particular house in Damascus. Ananias was not sure he had heard God right. He, a Christian whom Saul was trying to kill, was to visit Saul? He asked God about this, and God said yes, this was the man He was sending him to see.

Ananias was very afraid, but he had to obey God. God told him that Saul was blind, and that he should go and pray for him so he could see again. That was strange, but Ananias always did what God told him to do. So, he left his house and went to find Saul.

If you were Ananias, would you do this?

How would you feel and why?

Day 159 - Prayer

F ather in Heaven, thank You for You are a good God. Please make me an obedient servant who will always do what You tell me. When I am afraid to obey You, give me the courage to go, knowing that You are with me. Make me brave enough to tell my friends and others about You. Thank You, Lord, for giving me a heart that obeys Your Word. In Jesus' name. Amen.

Day 160 - Saul Waits on God

With a trembling heart, Ananias made his way through the streets of Damascus. He would see a man known for hunting down Christians like him. But God said he should go, so he was on his way.

In the meantime, Saul was in the house of Judas, wondering what was going to happen to him. It has now been three days since he fell off his horse and went blind. Since then, he had had nothing to eat or drink. He had also heard the voice of Jesus telling him to go into the city and wait for a man to come to him. Through this man, he would get back his sight. All this was very weird, but there was nothing Saul could do but wait.

Sometimes, we, too, have to learn to wait for what God has promised us.

If you were Saul, how would you feel now?

Day 161 - Prayer

Dear God, thank You because You are always with me. Lord, even when something terrible happens to me, You are there with me. Thank You for this and let me learn to pray and wait on You to help me because I know You always will. Thank You for that. In Jesus' name. Amen.

Day 162 – Saul can See Again

O bedient Ananias went to the house of Judas and found Saul. The two of them were not sure exactly what was going on, but God had spoken to them. So, Ananias prayed for Saul, just as God told him to do. Immediately, Saul's eyes opened, and he could see again.

That was not all. Saul changed his heart about Jesus while waiting for Ananias to come. When Ananias finished praying for Saul, Saul asked to be baptized. That meant he now believed that Jesus Christ was the Son of God and the world's Savior. That was wonderful, good news.

He no longer wanted to chase and capture Christians, and he was now one of them. Later, Saul changed his name to Paul and wrote many of the books in the New Testament. God certainly knows how to help us believe in Him.

Do you believe that Jesus Christ is the Son of God?

Do you also want to become a follower of Jesus, like Ananias and Paul?

Day 163 - Prayer

Dear Father, thank You for Your loving-kindness. I always want to be with Your Son, Jesus, because He is kind, good, and loving. He promised to get a place ready for me so that I could live with Him one day, and I can't wait for that to happen. Thank You, my Father, for loving me this much. In Jesus' name. Amen.

Day 164 - Jesus Blesses the Children

J esus was going all over Israel, preaching and teaching. Huge crowds of men, women, and children followed Him. Some wanted to hear what He was teaching. Others wanted Him to heal their sicknesses, and some only wanted to see Him.

One day, some women wanted Him to bless their children. These women and their children pushed their way to the front of the crowd, but the disciples would have none of it. They began chasing away the women and their children. When Jesus saw this, He stopped them. He asked the women to bring their children to Him. He took the children up in His arms and blessed all of them. The mothers and children were very happy. Jesus, the Son of God, had blessed them. Jesus wants all children to know that He loves them and wants to bless them. Receive His blessings today!

Do you know Jesus wants you to be with Him all the time?

Do you know He knows your name and the number of the hair on your head?

Day 165 - Prayer

Dear God, thank You for Your only Son, Jesus Christ. I believe that Jesus Christ is Your Son, and that He came into the world as a baby, just like me. He is no longer a baby. He is my Savior, and He wants to bless me. I receive His blessing today. I also receive His gift of life to me, and I receive Him into my heart. Thank You, because even if I am a child, He is with me. In Jesus' name. Amen.

Conclusion

W ow! We made it! I thank you for finishing this book with me. It was a wonder going through all the stories and prayers. I believe you have learned a lot. Keep it up! Would you please consider some of my other books so that we can continue this journey together? I can't do this without you, you know?

Please consider ordering one if you did not start with our Old Testament Amazing Moments storybook. It has 200 days of either a story or a prayer, and it also has a coloring book to go with it.

This book is the very first in a series for children. The next will be for children eight years and older, and it has stories and prayers for the same day, meaning with that book, you will be praying every day. I encourage you to purchase the other one. Check our Amazon store, and you will find ways I can help you in your walk with God.

I would love to see many other children taught God's truths in their homes. If I was valuable to you in that way, please leave an honest review on Amazon, and other parents will be encouraged to teach their children about God—with my help.

God bless you and yours! In Jesus' name. Amen!

Only One Life!

Resources

Youversion. (1996). [Computer software]. Life Church. https://www.youversion.com/the-bible-app/

Also By Only One Life

Biblical Bedtime Stories for Kids: Old Testament Amazing Moments Pointing Your Children to God, Ages 4 – 8.

Biblical Bedtime Stories for Kids: 113 Old Testament Amazing Moments Pointing Your Children to God Coloring Book, Ages 4 – 8.

Biblical Questions and Answers for Smart Kids: Quizzes Focused on the Book of Genesis to Help Your Children Grow and Learn about God – Who He is, His Love, and His Relationship with Humanity.

Biblical Characters for Kids: Adventures of the Patriarchs God Wants Your Children to Know, Ages 7-12.

About Author

"Only One Life" writes with a heart to help children know and love God from an early age. Through simple stories and biblical truths, their books give parents and teachers tools to guide children toward faith in Jesus and a strong foundation that will last a lifetime. Each story is written to spark imagination, open conversation, and lead young readers closer to the God who loves them.

Learn, grow, and love God together...

BIBLICAL BEDTIME STORIES FOR KIDS

OLD TESTAMENT AMAZING MOMENTS;
POINTING YOUR CHILDREN TO GOD,
AGES 4 – 8.

Only One Life

Contents

INTRODUCTION

This book of biblical stories is a stand-alone book. But you can combine it with the 'Biblical Bedtime Stories for Kids - New Testament Amazing Moments; Pointing Your Children to God,' and you will have 365 stories or prayers that will take each family through an entire year of walking with God. To visualize the stories in this book, we made a corresponding coloring book ... '113 Old Testament Amazing Moments: Pointing Your Children To God Coloring Book,' to complement the stories from this book. The New Testament Amazing Moments also has a coloring book to merge with.

It is intended for parents to read with their children, which is one of the first steps towards instilling the knowledge of God and His Word into their hearts. Proverbs 2:6 says to parents, "Train up a child in the way he should go, And when he is old, he will not depart from it." Also, Deuteronomy 6:6-7 further emphasizes that "...these words which I command you today shall be in your heart. You shall teach them diligently to your children, and shall talk of them when you sit in your house, when you walk by the way, when you lie down, and when you rise up." For us parents to diligently teach our children the scriptures with every opportunity we have - when we get up, sit at home, walk along the road, and in the evenings as Deuteronomy instructed - we need to follow a structured plan that is easy to follow. That is where this book comes in handy.

Paul reminded Timothy how, from childhood, he had known the Scriptures that made him wise unto salvation and which were no doubt taught to him by his mother and grandmother, stalwarts in the faith. We want to assist parents in this most crucial area! One of the motivating factors we wrote this book is to help parents do just this.

There are 200 days of either stories or prayers to help each family connect with God continuously. The objective is for parents to read one prayer or story per day and use this as a basis for teaching their children about God - who He is, what He is like, His relationship with humanity, and His moral rules for everyday living.

The stories in this book come from the Old Testament, and they are arranged primarily chronologically, allowing parents to fill in the gaps and impart their knowledge as needed. Doing so should develop a bigger overall picture of God's plan for humankind in the hearts of our young ones. Hopefully, this will also create a more cohesive view of God and His comprehensive plan for humanity.

We wrote the prayers to encourage children to pray regularly, thanking God, expressing their feelings for Him, and talking to Him as their Heavenly Father. The prayers are linked to the Bible stories and focus on an idea or lesson from the story. Expanding and providing additional explanation and background information to our kids is expected when necessary, with the knowledge of the Bible that we have.

Repetition has been said to reinforce existing skills, internalize concepts, and strengthen the brain's neural processors. That means repetition is a proven way for children of this age to learn better. That is why we structured the book to have days of stories and prayers separately. We encourage parents to individualize the stories for their kids for better retention on the prayer days. Doing that will remind the kids why they are praying the way they are since we connected the prayers to the stories.

By the end of the book, the kids should feel comfortable approaching God and talking to Him about anything. How awesome!

A particular emphasis is placed on being thankful. In addition, we stress using the name of Jesus to end each prayer. This will teach the children how to use the most potent name – Jesus- and lay a foundation for a praying life, based on the Scriptures. After His resurrection, Jesus told His disciples that all authority and power had been given unto Him, and they were to do everything, evoking His name. Jesus said, "...whatever you ask in My name, that I will do, that the Father may be glorified in the Son. If you ask anything in My name, I will do it" (John 14:13-14). What a tremendous promise!

The idea is for the parent to choose a particular time each day to share the stories with their children; we suggest before bed. That will help them to think about the wonders and glory of God before they fall asleep. The stories are told in simple, but engaging language suited to the age of the readers, yet remaining true to the Scriptures. The stories cover the full range of themes in the Bible.

Another objective of our books is to build in the child a rich treasury of Bible truths that reveal God and His ways, humanity's origin and our relationship with Him, His love for us as sinners, and His provision of salvation for us.

We encourage parents and guardians to read and discuss the stories and prayers with their children. Going through the book should help the children develop God's view versus a worldview based on the Bible. That is why we started with Creation, the Fall, man being driven from the garden, the Tower of Babel, the Flood, and what happened after that.

Central to the writing of this book is the belief that all humans are sinners and need the Savior and that there is only one way of salvation – through faith in Jesus Christ, God's Son. Others may view the stories as moral teachings, which no doubt they are. Still, the primary purpose of producing this book rests on the fact that we believe children and adults need the Savior by putting their faith in the Lord Jesus Christ. That is because we know, "That if you confess with your mouth the Lord Jesus and believe in your heart that God has raised him from the dead, you will be saved" Romans 10:9. Praise God! It doesn't matter if they are young. The Lord wants hearts that will believe in Him and a mouth that will confess Him.

We pray God's blessings on you and your family as you go on this learning journey. In Jesus' name. Amen!

DAY 1 – GOD MADE EVERYTHING

There was no land, sea, or sky before the world began. Everywhere was dark. On the first day, God said, "Let there be light!" He gave light the name, day, and the darkness He named night.

On the second day, He made the blue sky. God made the dry land, the sea, the grass, and the trees on the third day. He made the stars, moon, and sun on the fourth day. On the fifth day, God created all the creatures that live in the sea and the birds. On the sixth day, God then made all the land animals. Then, He made people. God saw that everything He made was very good.

So, He rested on the seventh day.

DAY 2 – PRAYER

Thank You, God, for making the heavens, earth, sun, moon, and stars I see in the sky. Thank You for making the bees that buzz and the birds that sing. Thank You for the deep blue sea and the soft gentle breeze. Thank You for the rain that goes pitter-patter on the roof. Thank You for the beautiful rainbow that stretches across the sky. Thank You, God, for making everything. And above all, thank You, my Father, for making my family and me. In Jesus' name. Amen.

DAY 3 – ADAM AND EVE IN THE GARDEN

God made Adam and Eve, and then He put them in charge of the beautiful garden. Here, there was no pain, sickness, sorrow, or death. Everything was perfect, and they were very happy. They had all the food they need-ed. But, in the garden, there was one tree that God told them not to eat from. It was the Tree of the Knowledge of Good and Evil.

One day, a snake told Eve she should eat the fruit because wonderful things would happen to her. Eve remembered what God said, but she believed the snake anyway. So, she ate the fruit then gave some to Adam. He ate it also. Immediately, they knew they had done something wrong by disobeying God's instructions. Because of this, God made them leave the lovely garden. Outside the garden, they lived in a world where there was pain, sickness, and death.

DAY 4 – PRAYER

Thank You, God, for a beautiful day today. Dear God, Adam and Eve did wrong when they listened to Satan. They disobeyed You. That is what sin is. Teach me always to do what You tell me. Thank You for being such a good teacher. In Jesus' name. Amen.

DAY 5 – CAIN AND ABEL

Adam and Eve had two sons. One was Cain, and the other was Abel. They grew up, and Cain became a farmer. Abel was a shepherd with lots of sheep. One day, the two of them brought gifts for God. Cain brought some of the things he grew on his farm. Abel brought his flocks' firstborn as well as their fat. God accepted Abel's gift. He did not accept Cain's produce from his farm.

Cain was very angry. God asked him, "Why are you angry? If you do well, what you do will be accepted. If you do not, sin is at your door."

But Cain did not answer. Instead, he killed Abel because God had accepted his gift. That was very wrong, and God punished Cain for doing it.

DAY 6 – PRAYER

Thank You, God, for my family. God, Cain did not like his brother Abel. That was why he hurt him. Hating someone can make you hurt them. Lord, keep me from hating anyone. I know You have answered me. Thank You for that. In Jesus' name. Amen.

DAY 7 – NOAH AND THE BIG BOAT

Noah was a righteous man who always did what God told him. But the other people he lived with loved doing bad things. They did not obey God and loved hurting each other. God was very unhappy with what they were doing. So, He decided to send a flood to punish them for being so bad. But God wanted to save Noah, and because Noah always obeyed Him, so he found favor in God's eyes. God told Noah to build a boat (ship, ark) to save himself and his family from the flood. As usual, Noah obeyed God and started building the boat.

It took Noah and his family a long time to finish making the boat. Many animals, two by two and some by seven, came into the boat when it was ready. After that, Noah and his family went inside, and God locked the door. Then, the rain began to fall and did not stop until it covered the whole earth. All the people outside the boat died.

God saved only Noah and his family because they found favor in his eyes.

DAY 8 – PRAYER

Thank You, dear God, for loving me so much that You sent Your Son Jesus to save me, just like You saved Noah from the flood. Thank You, Jesus, for obeying Your Father and coming to die for me. Thank You for coming into my tender heart and making me a child of God. Thank You, Father God, Holy Spirit, and Jesus, for making me a part of Your family. And thank You that one day I will live with You forever. In Jesus' name. Amen.

DAY 9 – NOAH'S RAINBOW

The rain fell for a long time while Noah, his family, and the animals were in the big boat. The boat sailed upon the waters for many days. One day, the rain stopped falling. The boat landed on the top of a mountain. But there was still a lot of water on the ground. As a result, Noah, his family, and all of the animals could not leave the ark.

After waiting a while, Noah sent a raven to fly around. The bird could not find anywhere to land, so it came back to the boat. Noah knew it was still not safe to go outside. After a few more days, Noah sent out a dove to look around. It came back with a leaf in its mouth. Now, Noah knew that the water was drying up from the earth.

Noah sent out another dove after waiting some more days, and the dove never came back. This time, Noah knew that the water had dried up enough that he, his family, and the animals could leave the boat. When Noah and his family finally came out of the boat, they were all so happy. They thanked God for saving them. Then God placed a rainbow in the sky. That was to remind Noah of God's promise never to destroy the people on the earth again with a flood.

DAY 10 – PRAYER

Thank You, God, for making the beautiful rainbow that I see in the sky. It always comes after the rain. I like its many colors, and I sometimes wonder where it begins and ends. It seems to go on forever, just like You. And it reminds me that you will always keep Your promises. Thank You again. In Jesus' name. Amen.

DAY 11 – THE TOWER OF BABEL

There were lots of people living on the earth after the flood. They all spoke the same language. God told them not to stay together in one place. They were to spread out worldwide and live, but they did not want to live away from each other.

The people said, "Let us build a tower, with its top reaching way up into the clouds."

This way, if there was another flood, they would not die. So the people stayed together and started building a very high tower.

God saw the tower they were building and said, "These are disobedient people. They have not spread all over the earth as I told them. Let's mix up their language and make them scatter all over the earth to live."

And so it happened that the people did not understand what the others were saying. So, all the people who spoke the same language got together and lived in a different part of the earth. That was how people began speaking different languages and went to live all over the earth. Wow! We know. Cool, ha?

DAY 12 – PRAYER

Thank You, God, for removing my stony heart and giving me a heart of flesh as You promised me in the Bible. Teach me, Lord, to always hear and obey Your Word. Let me not be stubborn and disobedient like these people were. Give me ears that hear Your Word and a heart that follows You so that I might please You and receive Your blessings. I bless Your name, for You are a good God. In Jesus' name. Amen.

DAY 13 – ABRAM LEAVES HIS HOME

Once there was a man named Abram living in a place called Ur. Here, the people did not worship Jehovah, the only true God. One day, God spoke to Abram.

He said, "I want you to leave your country, your family, and go to a place I will show you."

Abram was very surprised that God knew his name. He was a bit scared because God told him to go to a place he did not know. But Abram decided to obey God anyway. He packed up everything and left Ur.

God led him to a place called Canaan. It was a very good land, and the Lord blessed Abram greatly. He also changed his name to Abraham.

Sometimes, God can ask us to do hard things, but He always blesses us when we obey Him.

DAY 14 – PRAYER

Lord, I thank You because I know You have great things planned for my life. Father God, help me with the courage to do the things You ask me to do. Let me be brave like Abraham, who left everything he knew to go to a new place, just because You told him to do this. Please help me not to let my family or friends keep me from doing what You want me to do. Thank You again in Jesus' name. Amen.

DAY 15 – ABRAHAM AND LOT GO AWAY FROM EACH OTHER

When Abraham left Ur to go to Canaan, he took his nephew, Lot, with him. Lot's father had died, and Abraham brought him up like his son. They loved each other. When Abraham came to Canaan, he and Lot lived together. Both of them had a lot of sheep and cows. The space became too small to hold the animals belonging to the two of them. There was strife between Abraham and Lot's servants. Abraham, as a man of God, wanted peace. He did not want any fights between them.

To stop the quarrels, he told Lot it was best if they lived away from each other. Lot chose to go where the land was green and beautiful, and Abraham let him do this. So, they said goodbye and parted.

Abraham hated to see Lot go, but this was the best way to keep them from hurting each other. Abraham chose the path of peace that God loves.

DAY 16 – PRAYER

Thank You, dear God, for everyone that wants to make peace all over the world. Father God, help me to be a peacemaker, too. Let me be someone who tries to keep a quarrel from happening by speaking kind words and being ready to do what I can to stop the fuss. Please help me to be patient and kind to those who seek a quarrel with me. Thank You for helping me with that. In Jesus' name. Amen.

DAY 17 – ABRAHAM SAVES LOT

When Lot parted from his uncle, Abraham, he went to live in Sodom. Abraham always prayed for Lot and hoped he was doing alright. One day, a servant came and told Abraham that some kings had made war on Sodom. They had carried away Lot and his family as slaves.

Abraham was very sad to hear this because he loved Lot. He did not want anything bad to happen to him. So, he and his men went off to find Lot and bring him back to his home. They attacked the enemy's camp and rescued Lot and his family. Lot was very happy to be home again. He thanked his uncle for coming to save him.

Abraham might have said with a smile on his face, "That's alright, Lot. When you love somebody, you always try to help them."

DAY 18 – PRAYER

I thank You, Lord, for rescuing me from my worst foe, Satan, by dying on the cross for me. You loved me enough to come and rescue me from the devil. Help me never forget this. Help me to show my love for what You did by staying faithful to You all my life. Thank You for the answer. In Jesus' name. Amen.

DAY 19 – DON'T MOCK OTHERS

Have you ever been teased? How does it make you feel?

This is the true story of two brothers and what happened when one teased the other. Before Isaac was born, Abraham had another son named Ishmael. He was Isaac's big brother. On a special day when they had a party for Isaac, Ishmael was there, too. He was jealous of Isaac, and so he teased and laughed at him. That was not a very kind thing to do.

Sarah saw Ishmael laughing at Isaac, and it made her very upset. In the end, Abraham punished Ishmael by sending him away for doing this. We should never tease others because it hurts them.

DAY 20 – PRAYER

Lord, I praise You for being so good to me. God, please help me not to tease others because it hurts. I get upset when others tease me, and sometimes, it makes me cry. I don't want to do this to someone else because I don't like it for myself. Thank You for helping me not to mock others in Jesus' name. Amen.

DAY 21 – ABRAHAM AND ISAAC

Abraham and his wife Sarah were married for a long time. But they did not have any children. God had promised them that one day, they would have a son. But many years passed, and they still did not have a son. They wondered if God had forgotten about His promise to them. They kept praying for a son.

After many years had passed, Abraham and Sarah had given up hopes and thought it was already too late for them to have a son. One day, the Lord appeared unto Abraham. God told Abraham that he and Sarah would have a son very soon. Sarah was inside the tent and laughed when she heard this. She thought she was too old to have a child. But the next year, she had a son, just as God had promised. Abraham called him Isaac, and he and Sarah were very happy. They now knew that God always keeps His promises.

DAY 22 – PRAYER

Thank You, God, for all the many promises You have given to me in the Bible. God, help me to believe the promises that I find in it. Some of them seem impossible, but with You, everything is possible. Jesus, Your Son, calmed the winds on the sea, He raised the dead, and He made the blind to see. All these things tell me that You are a great, strong, and mighty God. Hallelujah! In Jesus' name. Amen.

DAY 23 – ESAU AND JACOB

I saac grew up, got married, and had two sons named Esau and Jacob. They were twin brothers, but they were always fussing. One day, Jacob bought Esau's birthright for a bowl of stew because Esau was hungry. Another time, Jacob pretended to be Esau to get his blessing from their father. Esau was very angry with Jacob and planned to kill him. So, Jacob left home and went to a far country to live. He stayed there for many years until God told him to return home. Jacob was still afraid of his brother. He did not know if he had forgiven him for what he had done to him. But Jacob obeyed God and set out to go back home. He asked God to make Esau forgive him.

As Jacob got near his home in Canaan, he saw his brother with many men coming to meet him. Jacob trembled with fear as Esau came nearer. But when Esau saw him, he ran and hugged him, instead of fighting with him. They forgave each other for the wrong things they had said and done. Jacob was happy.

God had heard and answered Jacob's prayer. That was so good because God wants us to forgive and live in peace with each other.

DAY 24 – PRAYER

Thank You, O God, for forgiving me my sins. Teach me, God, how to forgive those who hurt me. It is not easy to do this at all. I get so upset, and I want to get back at them. But Your Word says we are to forgive those who treat us unkindly and to pray for them. Thank You, for I know You have given me the power to do this. In the name of Jesus, I pray. Amen.

DAY 25 – JOSEPH AND HIS BROTHERS

Jacob had twelve children, and one of them was Joseph. His family called him a dreamer because he was always telling them about his dreams. Jacob adored Joseph more than any of his other brothers. He gave him a special coat of many colors to show how much he loved him. His ten brothers did not like this at all. So, they decided to get rid of Joseph.

One day, they threw Joseph into a deep hole. Then, they sold him to some people going to Egypt. His brothers knew that what they were doing was not right. Joseph begged them not to do this to him, but they did not listen. So, off he went to faraway Egypt to be a servant. But Joseph prayed to God to help him. God kept Joseph safe in Egypt. Both good and bad things happened to Joseph before he saw his brothers again.

We will find out what happened to him in the following few stories.

DAY 26 – PRAYER

Thank You, God, for giving me a loving family. God, I do not like being away from home. When I'm away from my family, I miss them terribly. But thank You, God, that wherever I go, You are still with me. In Jesus' name. Amen.

DAY 27 – JOSEPH HELPS A PRISONER

In Egypt, one day, Joseph found himself in prison. He had not done anything wrong. Somebody had lied about him, and so they locked him up. Joseph was very sad. But he still obeyed God and did what was right. He was also kind to the other prisoners around him.

One night, a prisoner had a strange dream. He was a butler, sent to prison by Pharaoh, the ruler of Egypt. The dream scared him and made him unhappy. Kind Joseph saw his sad face and asked him what was wrong. He told him about the dream. Joseph told him to cheer up. The dream meant that Pharaoh was not mad with him anymore. He was going to request for him soon.

A few days later, just as Joseph told him, Pharaoh did send for the butler. The butler thanked Joseph for being so kind to him. Joseph asked the butler to tell Pharaoh that he had not done anything wrong and shouldn't be in prison. "So, tell Pharaoh to please let me out," said Joseph to the butler.

The butler promised that he would do so. Joseph felt that God would answer his prayer very soon, and he would be out of prison.

Do you think the butler kept his promise to Joseph when he left the prison?

DAY 28 – PRAYER

God, I thank You for Your goodness upon my family and me. Please help me to be good to others even when I am not feeling happy myself. Let me think about them and try to help them. That is what Joseph did, and You blessed him. Bless me too, God. Thank You, Father, for I know You are a good God. In Jesus' name. Amen.

DAY 29 – JOSEPH MOVED FROM PRISON TO PALACE

Joseph had to wait a while after the butler left before he got out of prison. But he never stopped praying to God and doing what was right. One day, some guards from Pharaoh's palace came to fetch him. They made him bathe and change his clothes. Then they quickly took him to meet Pharaoh. Joseph was scared but also feeling glad.

At last, God was about to answer his prayer to get out of prison. Pharaoh had several dreams that bothered him. That was when the butler remembered how Joseph had told him the meaning of his dream. He told Pharaoh about Joseph, and that's why the king sent for him. Pharaoh now asked Joseph to tell him the meaning of his dreams. After seven years of abundant food, Joseph warned Pharaoh that Egypt would experience a seven-year famine. If Pharaoh did not do something about this, then the Egyptian people would die of hunger.

Pharaoh was worried by this news and asked Joseph what to do. He told Pharaoh to store up food during the years when there was plenty of food for the time when there would be very little food. Pharaoh thought this was a very good idea, and he put Joseph in charge of all the food. Now, he was the second ruler in Egypt, after Pharaoh, and he would never have to go back to prison again! Hallelujah! God had answered his prayer after all this time.

DAY 30 – PRAYER

Thank You, dear God, because You always answer our prayers even though sometimes, we have to wait for a while, like Joseph. Please help me learn to wait on You until You answer me before running off and doing something myself. I must remember that Your ears are always open to the prayers of Your children, and You will answer us. Thank You for giving me that knowledge. In Jesus' name. Amen.

DAY 31 – JOSEPH MEETS HIS BROTHERS AGAIN

D o you remember how Joseph's brothers had sold him into Egypt? His brothers never thought they would see him again. Now, Joseph was a ruler in Egypt and had a lot of power. The famine came, just as he had told Pharaoh it would. But the famine was also in Canaan, where Joseph's family lived. So, his father, Jacob, sent his brothers to Egypt to buy food.

As soon as Joseph's brothers arrived, Joseph knew who they were. But they did not know Joseph because it had been such a long time. He was dressed like an Egyptian and no longer looked like them; he even spoke like an Egyptian. Joseph remembered how mean they had been to him. Should he treat them the same way now? But Joseph loved his brothers, even though they had been so unkind to him. He also wanted to please God, who tells us to forgive those who hurt us. So, Joseph told them that he was their brother after playing some tricks on them. They could not believe it. They became afraid he would hurt them. But Joseph told them that he loved them and had forgiven them.

They were so surprised and glad. Joseph gave them all the food they needed and sent them to fetch their father so they could all live together in Egypt. They became one big happy family because Joseph forgave them for wanting to hurt him. That is how God also forgives us for the wrong things we do.

DAY 32 – PRAYER

Thank You, O God, for forgiving me my sins. Teach me, O God, to forgive those who hurt me. I know this is a very tough thing to do, especially when they are not sorry. Fill my tender heart with Your love so that I can forgive them. Thank You for helping me in this area. In Jesus' name. Amen.

DAY 33 – GOD SAVES BABY MOSES

Joseph's brothers and their families went to live in Egypt. After many, many years, they had lots of children. God had changed Jacob's name to Israel, so all of his descendants were called Israelites. Because there were so many Israelites, Pharaoh was afraid they would take over the country. So, he told his soldiers to kill every baby boy born to the Israelites by throwing them into the river. The mothers were scared and did everything they could to keep their babies safe.

Moses' mother was a very wise woman. When she had Moses, she kept him hidden from Pharaoh's soldiers for three months. When she could not hide the baby anymore, she made a basket and put him in it. She asked God to keep him alive because he was a good baby. Then, she put the basket in the bushes by the side of the water. Miriam, Moses' sister, stood nearby to watch the basket with the baby in it. When Pharaoh's daughter came to the river to bathe, she saw the basket. She opened it and saw Moses, who was crying. Pharaoh's daughter took Moses to her house as her child. That saved him from Pharaoh's soldiers.

DAY 34 – PRAYER

God, You are a good God that watches over us from the day we are born. You knew all about Moses and what Pharaoh was trying to do to him. But, You had a plan for him, and so You saved his life. Let me remember that You have a plan for my life, too. All I need to do is trust You and Your plan for me. Thank You for always thinking about me. In Jesus' name. Amen.

DAY 35 – MOSES IN THE PALACE

Moses grew up in Pharaoh's palace as his grandson. But he was actually a Hebrew, an Israelite. His people were slaves in Egypt, yet, he lived like a prince. As a young man, he saw an Egyptian beating an Israelite. Moses got angry with the Egyptian. He quickly looked around to see if anyone was watching. He did not see anyone, so he killed the Egyptian for trying to hurt an Israelite. Then Moses buried him in the sand.

Another day, he went out and saw two men fighting. This time, they were both Israelites. Moses told them to stop fighting with each other because they were brothers.

One of them asked Moses, "Do you want to kill me like the Egyptian the other day?"

Moses was scared. People knew he had killed the Egyptian. Someone went and told Pharaoh, and he began looking for Moses to punish him. Moses was in big trouble. So, he ran far away from Egypt and went to live in Midian.

Was this the end of Moses? No, because God had a very important job for him to do.

DAY 36 – GOD CALLS MOSES

Moses lived in Midian for forty years. There he married one of Jethro's daughters and had two sons. He was a shepherd and looked after Jethro's sheep. Back in Egypt, Pharaoh kept mistreating the Israelites. He made them work very hard as slaves. They suffered because of this and prayed to God for help. God heard their prayers and decided to answer them. One day, he appeared to Moses in a bush that burned brightly with fire. Moses was frightened and wondered how the bush just kept burning, and the fire did not go out. He went nearer to look at it closely.

Then God spoke to him, and He said, "Moses, I want you to go and tell Pharaoh to free the Israelites, so they will no longer be slaves."

Moses was surprised to hear this and very afraid. If he went back to Egypt, Pharaoh might kill him. He also knew that Pharaoh would never let his people go free.

What should he do? Obey God or stay in Midian?

DAY 37 – PRAYER

Thank You, God, for providing for my parents to buy this book for me. Lord God, You always want us to obey You, but it is not always easy. Please help me to trust You, so I will do what You tell me. Thank You because I know You always answer me whenever I pray. In Jesus' name. Amen.

DAY 38 – MOSES OBEYS GOD

G od told Moses, "Go back to Egypt."

Moses was to be God's messenger to Pharaoh. He was to tell Pharaoh to let the Israelite slaves go free. Moses did not want to go because he was not a good speaker. God sent Moses' brother, Aaron, so he could help him talk to Pharaoh.

When they told Pharaoh what God said, he was very upset. He did not agree to let the Israelites go free from being slaves. Instead, he made them work even harder.

God sent Moses and Aaron back to Pharaoh. Moses told Aaron to throw down a stick, and it became a snake. Pharaoh laughed and let his magicians do the same. But then, Moses' snake ate up Pharaoh's snakes. That showed that God was greater than Pharaoh. But still, Pharaoh would not let the Israelites go free.

We will find out what God did next.

DAY 39 – PRAYER

Lord, thank You because You are a good God. Father God, You call every one of Your children to come to You. Let me hear Your voice calling me, and let me not be afraid when I hear it. Now that I am Your child, let me learn that You will also give me the power to do something when You tell me to do it. I believe You are greater than anyone else. You can do the things You say You will do for us. Thank You, my Father and God. In Jesus' name. Amen.

DAY 40 – MOSES AND HIS PEOPLE LEAVE EGYPT

Moses kept telling Pharaoh that God said he was to set the Israelites free from slavery. But Pharaoh would not listen. He did not want to obey God. Every time Moses spoke to him, he said no. God wanted to show Pharaoh that it was not good to disobey Him. Each time Pharaoh did not do what God said, something amazing happened.

They called that a miracle because only God could do it.

For example, God turned all the water in Egypt into blood. No one had any water to drink for seven days.

Another time, He sent lots of frogs that went, "Croak! Croak!"

Then many flies, "Bzzz, Bzzz!" came upon the land. They were everywhere, and the people were afraid of them.

The people begged Pharaoh to obey God and let His people go. But still, Pharaoh would not do it. The land became dark for many days, many animals died, and sores came upon them and the people. But Pharaoh was very stubborn. He still said, "No," to God's command. Only after Pharaoh's son and many other Egyptian children died did he decide to obey God. At last, he told the Israelites to leave. Moses and his people were very happy to get away from Egypt.

They thanked God for setting them free.

DAY 41 – PRAYER

Thank You, Lord, for saving me. Thank You, dear Lord, for forgiving me of all my sins. Thank You, Lord, for making me Your child. Thank You, Lord, for preparing a place in Heaven for me. I want to thank You, Lord, in Jesus' name. Amen!

DAY 42 – GOD KEEPS HIS PROMISES TO ABRAHAM

T he children of Israel were very happy to leave Egypt. They were no longer slaves to Pharaoh. They took their animals and everything that they had with them. They were going to the promised Land of Canaan God had given to their fathers Abraham, Isaac, and Jacob a long time ago. Jacob was the one who had twelve sons. These were Joseph and his eleven brothers who came into Egypt. God had changed Jacob's name to Israel, and so his children were called Israelites.

They grew to a very large number in Egypt. These were the ones who had now left Egypt. They sang praises to God as they went on their way to Canaan. God had kept His promises to Abraham, Isaac, and Jacob – to give them the Land of Canaan to live in.

The Israelites now knew that God never forgets His people, no matter what happens.

DAY 43 – PRAYER

I want to praise You, Lord, for what You have done for me. You brought me into Your kingdom. You have blessed me with many good things. You are always with me to protect and keep me safe. And, one day, I know I will be living with You forever. Praise ye the name of the Lord! In Jesus' name. Amen.

DAY 44 – PHARAOH CHASES AFTER THE ISRAELITES

After the people left Egypt, stubborn Pharaoh changed his mind. He wanted the Israelites to come back and be slaves again.

Oh wow!

Aha, he had no one to do all his work for him now that the Israelites were gone. So, he and his army of soldiers ran after the freed Israelites to bring them back to be his slaves again. The Israelites were in the desert when they saw Pharaoh's chariots coming for them. They were very scared.

They called out to Moses, "What must we do? Pharaoh is coming to kill us!"

One of them said, "We have nowhere to go."

"The mountains are on two sides of us, Pharaoh is behind us, and the Red Sea is before us," yelled another man.

"We're all going to die!" shouted the people.

But Moses believed God and asked Him what to do. God told Moses to stretch out his stick over the sea. When he did this, an amazing thing happened. The sea opened up, and a road appeared in the middle of the water. All the Israelites quickly rushed onto the road and crossed over to the other side. Pharaoh and his army followed them, but the sea came back together and drowned them all. God delivered Israel entirely from Pharaoh.

God always helps His people when they obey Him.

DAY 45 – PRAYER

God, thank You because You are the one who delivers us from our enemies. We do not have to fight them ourselves. We only have to pray to You and trust You to do the work. It does not matter how mighty the things that scare us are. You are always on our side to deliver us. Thank You, Lord! In Jesus' name. Amen.

DAY 46 – GOD TAKES CARE OF HIS PEOPLE

The Israelites continued their trip to Canaan. Pharaoh could not trouble them again. The desert was a very hot and dry place. There was not a lot of water or food around. The food they took from Egypt was almost gone.

"We're hungry," they said to Moses.

"We're always thirsty, and the sun is so hot," they said.

"Yes, and the nights are cold," cried others.

When they were hungry, God sent food from heaven for them to eat. While they were sleeping, God made small white bits of bread fall from heaven. That was called manna, which they ate like bread. For water, God made it flow out of a big rock when Moses hit it with a stick. Only God could make these things happen. He was very good to His people. He gave them these things just as they needed them.

DAY 47 – PRAYER

Lord, thank You, for You are the God that takes care of us. You give us food, clothes and somewhere to live. You bless us with parents who love and look after us. You said we must not worry about these things because You already know we need them. Help me to stop being anxious and trust You. Thank You again. In Jesus' name. Amen.

DAY 48 – MOSES, AARON, AND HUR WORKING TOGETHER

Many people tried to keep the Israelites from getting into the land God had promised them. The Amalekites were one of them. They came to fight against the children of Israel. The people were afraid, but God told Moses what to do. He told him to go up on a hill and hold up his stick in his hand. Whenever Moses held up his hand, Israel began winning the war. But whenever Moses' hands grew tired, and he let them down, the Amalekites started winning.

Yikes, this was not good at all!

Then Aaron and Hur came up the hill and helped to keep Moses' hands in the air. Moses' hands never came down again, and Israel won the war.

That is what happens when people work together to do what God tells them.

DAY 49 – PRAYER

Lord, thank You because You are a good God. God, You tell Your children to do Your work together, and things will go well. Dear God, sometimes I like to fuss with others, and I want to do things all by myself. Help me, God, learn how to work with others to do what You want us to do. Help me to understand that things are easier and go better when we work together in love. Thank You, my Father, in Jesus' name. Amen.

DAY 50 – MOSES' FAMILY COMES TO VISIT HIM

When Moses was in Midian, he was married. His wife's name was Zipporah, and he had two sons, Gershom and Eliezer. When Moses came back to Egypt, he took his wife and children with him. Later, he sent them back to Midian. Moses missed his family very much. Now that they were traveling in the desert, he longed to see them, but he was too busy looking after the people every day. He did not have any time to go back to Midian for them.

One day, someone told him that his father-in-law had come to visit him. Moses went out of his tent. There before him was his wife, two children, and his father-in-law. He ran and hugged them. Moses was so happy. He thanked God for bringing his family back together again.

DAY 51 – PRAYER

T hank You, God, for my family, who love me so much. I want to thank You for their love, warm kisses, and how they take good care of me and teach me to know right from wrong. Thank You for the fun times we have together and how they cheer me up when I feel sad. I pray for children that do not have parents. Lord, provide someone to act as their faithful parent. Thank You, my Father, for being so good to me. In Jesus' name. Amen.

DAY 52 – GOD'S SPECIAL RULES

The Israelites traveled for many days in the desert.

One day, they came to a place called Mount Sinai. There, God spoke to Moses. He told him that He wanted to make Israel His special people. But for this to happen, they would have to agree to work together. God told them He would always bless them if they obeyed Him.

That sounded very good to the Israelites. They agreed to do whatever God told them. These were some of the things God told them to do. They should worship Him only as God and no one else. They were not to make any statues to worship. They were not to misuse His name in any way. They were to worship Him in a special way on the Sabbath Day. They were to honor and obey their parents. They should not kill, commit adultery, or steal. Lastly, He told them not to lie or to envy people for what they had.

These were the rules the Israelites were to follow, and God would bless them.

DAY 53 – PRAYER

Thank You, Father, because You are always thinking about my wellbeing. Dear God, help me to remember why You give us rules. You give them to us because You love us and want to keep us safe. When we break Your rules, we hurt ourselves and others. Keeping Your rules helps us enjoy Your many blessings. Help me remember this and obey Your rules, Lord. I am so grateful You care for me. In Jesus' name. Amen.

DAY 54 – ISRAEL BREAKS GOD'S SPECIAL RULES

God told Moses His ten special rules for Israel. But He wanted the people to remember them always. So, He called Moses up to the top of the mountain. No one else went with him. Then God wrote the Ten Rules (Commandments) on stone tablets. He gave them to Moses to take to the people.

For a solid forty days and nights, Moses was on top of the mountain getting the Ten Rules from God.

That was a very long time.

The people were not sure Moses was coming back. So, they had a party and worshipped another god. They also broke some of the other rules God gave them. When Moses was coming down from the mountain, he heard music and dancing. He came back to find out that the people had broken some of God's rules. That made God angry, and He was going to punish them. But Moses asked God not to do it but to forgive them. God listened to Moses, and He forgave the people.

God is a forgiving God.

DAY 55 – PRAYER

Thank You, our Father, for listening to our prayers and not always punishing us. When we do something wrong and say we are sorry, You forgive us. I love You for being like this. Thank You once more in Jesus' name. Amen.

DAY 56 – BE SATISFIED WITH WHAT GOD GIVES YOU

The Israelites were having a hard time as they journeyed to the land God had promised them. God sent them bread, called manna, to eat every day. He gave the Israelites water to drink, also. But, the people were tired of the bread. They wanted some meat to eat like they used to have in Egypt. So, they began fussing with Moses again.

"We want some meat," they said. "We're tired of eating only bread."

The Lord heard this and was upset with them. They were not thankful for what He was giving them. So, He caused a strong wind to blow, which brought many quails or small birds into the camp. The people gladly caught the birds and cooked them. But while some of them were eating the meat, they died. All this took place because they were not happy with what God had given to them.

DAY 57 – PRAYER

Lord, thank You for always giving me all that I need. God, You said we must be satisfied with what You give us. We should not murmur or complain but be thankful. This is not easy, especially when I want something else. But, God, help me to remember that You only give us what is good for us. Help me trust You more, be satisfied with what I have, and be grateful. Thank You for the answer in Jesus' name. Amen.

DAY 58 – GOD DOES NOT LIKE GOSSIP

When we gossip, we say unkind or untrue things about others. God does not like this at all. We find this out in the story about Miriam, Aaron, and their brother, Moses. God made Moses the leader of Israel. It seemed as if Aaron and Miriam did not like this. They wanted to be in charge, too. So, they said mean things about Moses. One of them was about the woman he married. She came from a different country.

God heard all that Miriam and Aaron were saying about Moses. He punished Miriam for speaking badly about her brother. God put big sores on her skin for many days, and Israel could not move on until it got better. She learned that God is upset when we say hurtful things about others.

DAY 59 – PRAYER

Thank you, Lord, for Your Word is always pointing me in the right direction. God, I love to gossip, and so do my friends. It is like a hobby every time we meet. We spend a lot of time talking about other people, and it is hardly anything good. Help me only to say what is good about others. Let me not say anything that may be untrue and not good. Let me say only kind things about others, as I would want them to say about me. Thank You, my God. In Jesus' name. Amen.

DAY 60 – THE PEOPLE MAKE A TEMPLE FOR GOD

G od told Moses to build a temple where the people could worship Him. The people were in the desert, so they did not have many things to make it with. But they loved God so much and wanted to show this to Him.

So, guess what they did?

The women took all their jewelry and gave it to Moses to help make the temple. Some brought pieces of cloth to make the curtains. Others used their skills and talents to make the pictures and other furniture. When they finished, they had a beautiful house for God, and He was very pleased.

Together the people gave what they had to build the house of God. They learned to work together to please God.

DAY 61 – PRAYER

Thank You, O God, for who You are. God, I want You to always stay with me. I cannot make You a temple or a house. But I am asking You to come and live in my heart. Let it become Your house. Thank You, God, for making my heart Your temple. In Jesus' name. Amen.

DAY 62 – A TALKING DONKEY

There was a man named Balaam. He was a prophet of God. He loved having lots of money.

One of Israel's enemies came and asked him to cast a spell on them. The king promised him a lot of money if he would do it. God told Balaam not to do it. But, because Balaam loved money, he wanted to do what the king asked. So, he saddled his donkey and set out to see the king.

On the way, God sent an angel to stop Balaam from going. But only the donkey saw the angel. The donkey stopped and would not go any further. Balaam got angry with the donkey and beat him with a stick.

God made the donkey talk, and it asked Balaam, "What have I done to you that you have struck me these three times?"

Balaam replied to his donkey that it had made a fool of him. The donkey told Balaam that it had always been loyal to him. Then God opened Balaam's eyes, and he saw the angel with a drawn sword, standing in their way. Balaam was frightened. The donkey had saved his life. The angel would have killed him if the donkey had not stopped.

God always wants to help us to obey Him. He always makes a way for us to come to Him because He is a good God!

DAY 63 – PRAYER

Thank You, Father, because Your voice always tells me when I leave Your ways, saying, "This is the way, walk in it."

Father God, help me not to love anything else more than You. Help me always to obey You and do what You want, not what I want to do. Give me an obedient heart. Thank You for making it possible. In Jesus' name. Amen.

DAY 64 – BELIEVE WHAT GOD TELLS YOU

After the Israelites journeyed in the desert for some months, they came to the border of Canaan. That was the land God had promised to give them. They were very excited. Soon, they would reach the end of their long journey. In Canaan, they would have houses to live in instead of tents. They would not have to keep moving from place to place. They would have land to farm, and they could feed their animals. They wouldn't be slaves to any nation. Things would be much better for them than it was in the desert.

God told Moses to send twelve men to go and look at the land to see what it was like. Moses chose one man from each of Israel's twelve tribes. The men traveled through the land and saw that it was a good place to live. But they also saw some giants and were very afraid.

Ten of them told Moses about the giants and that they should not go there. Two men, Joshua and Caleb, told them that God would help them overcome the giants. But the people didn't listen to Joshua and Caleb. They believed the giants would kill them. So, all the people said they would not go into Canaan, even though God told them to. Because of this, God made them stay in the desert for forty more years. There, life was very hard for them just because they did not obey God.

DAY 65 – PRAYER

Lord God, thank You because You know everything. God, let me not be afraid even when things look scary. You are always with me, and so You will help me. I can always trust in You because You are so big, strong, and mighty. Thank You for Your beautiful works. In Jesus' name. Amen.

DAY 66 – GOD TELLS MOSES 'NO'

Moses spent most of his life leading Israel to the Promised Land. He was the first person God told about His plan for Israel to leave Egypt and go to the land He had promised their fathers – Abraham, Isaac, and Jacob. It was not an easy job, but Moses did it with God's help.

Moses knew that Canaan, the Promised Land, was a good place to live. He wanted to go there, too. However, when it was time for Israel to go into the land, God told Moses he could not go with them.

He asked God, 'Why?'

Moses was very disappointed he could not go to Canaan with his people, for God reminded him that he had disobeyed Him before them. But, he was a humble man; therefore, he accepted what God said.

God does not always respond to our prayers in the way we wish, and we must learn to accept this and still trust Him, just as Moses did.

DAY 67 – PRAYER

Thank You, God, because I know You love me. God, I don't want to get mad when You don't answer my prayer the way I want it to be answered. It is hard to do this, but I believe You only give me what is good for me. Let me remember this and still praise You. Thank You, my Father. In Jesus' name. Amen.

DAY 68 – JOSHUA PLEASES GOD

Before Moses died, God chose a new leader for the Israelites. His name was Joshua. His name means savior. Joshua was such a brave young man and was a servant to Moses. He went part way up the mountain with Moses when Moses went to get the Ten Rules from God.

He did not worship idols like some of the other people. He loved God and liked staying in the house of God and learning about Him. Sometimes he led the army of Israel in war and won. He always obeyed whatever God said. God knew all this, and, He chose him as the new leader.

God is always watching us. He will bless us when we are good.

DAY 69 – PRAYER

Lord God, thank You for always watching over me. Father, I always want to do what makes You happy. I want You to bless me and keep looking out for me all the time. It is good to know that I have a Father in Heaven. Thank You for being my Father. In Jesus' name. Amen.

DAY 70 – JOSHUA AND THE BATTLE OF JERICHO

Jericho was in the Land of Canaan. The people who lived there were enemies of Israel. God told Joshua to go and capture Jericho for His people to live in. The city of Jericho had solid and very high walls to break down. But God told Joshua just what he had to do to get into the city. He told him to let the Israelites march around the city once each day. As they marched, they were not to say anything or make a noise. The children of Israel did that for six days.

The people of Jericho believed the Israelites were crazy for doing what they were doing. On the seventh day, God instructed Joshua to have the people march around the city seven times. The priests were to blow their trumpets loudly for the seventh time, and the people were to yell.

"Taptanaw! Taptanaw!" sounded the trumpets.

"Hurrah! Hurrah!" yelled the people.

"Crash!"

The noise from the trumpets and the yelling of the people made the big strong walls of Jericho fall flat. Israel took over the city, just as God had told them to.

When we trust God, He can work miracles for us.

DAY 71 – PRAYER

Lord, thank You for Your awesome power. God, I want to be a soldier in Your army. I will put on my helmet of salvation and my shield of faith. When someone says I can't do what You tell me, I will say, "Yes, I can!"

When they ask me why, I will say, "Because I am Your child, and You are always with me, so I can do everything because You give me power!"

Thank You, Most High God, for giving me the strength to do what You say. In Jesus' name. Amen.

DAY 72 – RAHAB AND HER FAMILY SAVED

N ow before Joshua began marching around Jericho, he sent two men to spy out the land. He wanted them to find out how many soldiers were there and how they could get inside the city. The two spies secretly entered the city, and they came to a woman's house. Her name was Rahab. She had heard about the mighty power of Israel's God, who had destroyed Pharaoh and his army in the Red Sea. She and all the people of Jericho were afraid of the Israelites because of this.

The King of Jericho was looking for the spies, to kill them. So, Rahab asked them if they would save her life and her family if she hid them from the king's soldiers. They said yes. So, Rehab hid them, and the soldiers did not find them. The men promised Rahab that they would come and get her and her family when they captured Jericho. They gave her a special red cord to hang in her window so they could find her house. When the walls of Jericho fell, the two spies came for Rahab. They saved her and her family, and they too started to believe in the true God of Israel.

DAY 73 – PRAYER

Lord, You are so kind to Your people. Rahab was a good woman because she took care of Your people. Help me always to help others who are in trouble. Lord, some of Your children are in trouble right now. Make an escape plan for them as You made for those two spies. Please bless me like You blessed Rahab for what she did. Thank You for always guiding Your children with love. In Jesus' name. Amen.

DAY 74 – STEALING IS WRONG

The next city that Joshua went to fight against was Ai. God told him that the people were to destroy everything they found in the city when they captured it. Everyone agreed to do what the Lord said. But there was one man named Achan who did not listen.

After Israel captured the city, he saw a beautiful golden coat that he wanted for himself. So, he took it and hid it in his tent so no one would know. God knew it was Achan and told Joshua. Achan could no longer keep what he had stolen a secret. God told them to punish him because he had disobeyed him.

Achan was very sorry, but it did not help. He still had to be punished for not obeying God.

DAY 75 – PRAYER

Thank You, God, because You know everything. God, I know stealing is wrong. Even when no one else sees me do it; you will. Please help me not to steal anything, big or small, from people. Also, God, keep my things safe from others that want to steal them from me. Thank You for the answer. In Jesus' name. Amen.

DAY 76 – JOSHUA FORGETS TO OBEY GOD

Joshua and the Israelites fought many wars and captured the land of Canaan. God told them not to make any agreements with the people in the land. That was because they worshipped other gods, and Jehovah did not want His people to do this. He was the only true God they were to worship. But Joshua did not remember this all the time. He forgot about this when the Gibeonites came to visit them. They told him that they came from a very far away land. They showed him their old bread, their dirty and torn old clothes. Joshua believed them and never asked God if what they said was true. He made an agreement with them.

It was when he finished making the agreement that he found out that they had lied to him. They came from the Land of Canaan that Israel was now in. But it was too late. Joshua had made a promise to them so he could not chase them out of the land. He had to let them live side by side with the Israelites, which caused them a lot of trouble because of their different ways.

That is why we must always listen and obey what God tells us.

DAY 77 – PRAYER

Thank You, O God, for always taking care of all the children in the world and me. Joshua got into trouble for not obeying You, God. I do not want this to happen to me. Teach me to obey Your Word, O Lord. Thank You for Your Word in the Bible that always guides us in the right direction. In Jesus' name. Amen.

DAY 78 – FAITHFUL JOSHUA

J oshua was a faithful servant of God all his life. He shows us how we are to love and serve God. He loved God and became His servant from when he was a very young man. He helped Moses guide the people all the time they were in the desert. He went with the eleven men to spy out the land. Only he and Caleb brought back a good report.

Joshua told them that they should not be afraid of the giants in Canaan. God would help them conquer those enemies. But the people did not believe them, and God let them wander around in the wilderness for forty more years. God kept Joshua alive all this time, and only he and Caleb from this group were allowed into the Promised Land. After Moses died, he became the leader, and he won almost every battle he fought for Israel because he did what God told him.

As he got old and was about to die, he spoke to the Israelites. He reminded them of all the good things God had done for them. He told them always to be faithful to God, no matter what happened.

That is how we must live, too.

DAY 79 – BRAVE CALEB

C aleb and Joshua were friends. The two of them always believed in and served God. They were the only two spies out of the twelve who brought good news after they spied out the Land of Canaan. But the people did not believe them, so God made them wander in the desert for another forty years. When it was time for the children of Israel to go into Canaan after this, only Caleb and Joshua from their group were still alive. God made sure of this because of their faith in Him.

When they entered Canaan, Caleb was eighty-five years old, but he was still very strong. So, he went to Joshua and asked him for his piece of land there. Giants lived in it, but it did not bother Caleb. He knew that God would help him overcome them. This is what happened. Caleb drove out three giants from Hebron and lived a long time after that.

When we believe God, He gives us the strength to do hard things.

DAY 80 – DEBORAH, A BRAVE WOMAN OF GOD

Israel's enemies were always fighting against them. When Israel got into trouble, they always asked God for help. Because He was their King and loving God, and they were His children, He always helped them. But they had to do what He told them. Now, they were in trouble again, with a man named Sisera.

God sent the leader of Israel's army to a woman named Deborah. She was a judge and a prophet in Israel. That means God gave her messages to give to the people. He also gave her wisdom to know what was right or wrong when there was a problem. Usually, only men were judges, but with God, Deborah was special. She was also very brave and went into the war with Israel. They won the battle, and they praised God.

They were all very thankful for brave Deborah, who went with them.

It does not matter if you are a boy or a girl – God can use you!

DAY 81 – PRAYER

Thank You, God, for I know You have great things ahead for me. Father God, I want to be used of You to do great things. Let me be like Moses or Deborah. They believed in You and did whatever You told them. When I grow up, I want to serve You with all my strength. Thank You, Father, for my future is bright. In Jesus' name. Amen.

DAY 82 – GIDEON: GOD'S MIGHTY WARRIOR

One day Gideon was busy preparing wheat for his family. He was hiding because of the Midianites. If they saw him, they would take his wheat away. The Midianites were Israel's enemies. Every day they came and stole their food and animals. The Israelites were very unhappy and asked God to help them.

Suddenly, an angel appeared to Gideon. He was afraid and wondered what he wanted. The angel told him that God had chosen him to deliver Israel from her enemies.

"But I am not a fighter," Gideon said. "I can't do it."

"Yes, you can," said the angel, "because God is with you."

"How can I do it?" asked Gedeon.

"Just do whatever God tells you," the angel said.

God told Gideon that he should gather an army to fight, but it was too large. Gideon sent home those who were afraid. Many men left, but the number was still too big. God had Gideon bring the number down to only three hundred men. Everybody wondered how so few of them were going to defeat the large army of the Midianites. But when God is with you, you can do impossible things. Gideon's three hundred men defeated their enemies because God was on their side.

DAY 83 – PRAYER

Lord, thank You very much for always being with us all the time. Father, Gideon won the battle because You were with him. Even though he was afraid, he did what You told him and trusted You to win the fight for him. Let me be brave like him, even when I am afraid because You are with me. Thank You for being there for me. In Jesus' name. Amen.

DAY 84 – SAMSON, THE STRONG MAN

Samson was a judge over Israel for many years. He heard from God and told people what to do when they had problems. But there was something very special about Samson. God made him a very strong man so he could help keep his people safe from their enemies.

Samson was so super strong that he killed a lion with only his hands. He used a jawbone from a donkey to fight off many soldiers who came to attack him. One morning, he woke up to find out that his enemies had locked him up in their city. They were waiting to kill him. Samson pulled down and carried off the huge gates of the city on his shoulders. His enemies could not catch him. He was like superman because he was so strong. Samson was safe as long as he obeyed God.

Would he stay safe for long?

Read the following story to find out.

DAY 85 – PRAYER

Thank You, O God, for Your wonderful works. Help me, dear Father, not to trust in my strength but to trust in You. Even if I feel strong, I still need You to help me overcome my enemy - the Devil. Let me never forget that I can do nothing without You. Thank You for hearing my prayers. In Jesus' name. Amen.

DAY 86 – SAMSON'S SPECIAL SECRET

C an you keep a secret and not tell anyone?

Is it easy or hard to do?

Well, Samson had a special secret about why he was so strong. Before he was born, God told his mother not to cut his hair. He was to let it grow long. If he ever cut it short, he would lose his strength. That was his secret, and he was to tell no one about it. So, Samson always kept his hair long.

Now, the Philistines were the enemies of Samson's people, and they mistreated them. Many times, Samson used his strength to help his people. The Philistines did not like this and tried to kill Samson. But no matter what the Philistines did, they could not stop him. He was too strong for them. This continued for quite some time until Samson did something he shouldn't have done.

Can you guess what this was?

Read the next story to find out.

DAY 87 – SAMSON SHARES HIS SECRET

W e know that Samson was a very strong man, and he had a secret about why this was so. He was strong because God told him not to cut his hair. His strength was in his long hair.

Samson's enemies, the Philistines, always wanted to get rid of him, but they could not. They made a plan to find out Samson's secret, so they could kill him when he was weak. They sent one of their women, Delilah, to play like she loved him. He did not know this and fell in love with her. Every day, she kept on asking Samson to tell her why he was so strong. He did not tell her his secret at first. But, as she kept asking and because he loved her, he finally told her that his strength was in his long hair. He also told Delilah that he was not to drink wine.

Delilah was so happy to hear this. That very night she made him drink wine, and she had Samson's hair cut off while he was sleeping. Then she sent and called her Philistine soldiers to come for Samson.

What do you think happened after that?

Tomorrow, you'll find out.

DAY 88 – SAMSON AND THE PHILISTINES

Delilah tricked Samson into telling his secret to her. Now she knew that his strength came from his long hair. So, she made Samson drink wine and called her people to come and cut off Samson's long hair. The Philistine soldiers did.

When Samson woke up, he tried to fight them off. But he was no longer strong because his hair was gone. They took him back to their country. There, they made him blind and turned him into a slave, grinding corn for them. Samson had disobeyed God, and now he found himself unhappy and in serious trouble. He cried and prayed to God every day, telling Him how sorry he was for not doing what He had said.

How he wished he had kept his secret to himself!

DAY 89 – GOD HEARS SAMSON'S PRAYER

S amson found himself living in the land of the Philistines. He was their slave and spent most of his time grinding corn for them. The people mocked him every day.

"Where is your strength now, Samson?"

"Do you remember how you were strong and mighty, and we were afraid of you?"

"Now, you are our slave. Ha! Ha! Ha!"

Samson felt very bad about this. If only he had been wise and not foolish. But every day, little by little, Samson's hair kept growing back. That meant that his strength was coming back.

One day, the Philistines had a great big gathering. They all gathered together in the temple of their god to celebrate it. They sent for Samson and made fun of him.

That day, Samson prayed to God and asked Him to make him strong one more time. God heard Samson's prayer, and he used his strength to pull down the huge temple. Many Philistines died that day. Samson died, too. On the day that Samson died, he killed more people than he did when he was alive.

For a long time, Israel was not bothered by the Philistines again.

DAY 90 – PRAYER

Thank You, God, that You still hear our prayers, and You will have mercy on us. You are ready to help us even when we are the ones who caused our own problems. That is very good of You, Lord. In Jesus' name. Amen.

DAY 91 – NAOMI LEAVES HOME

T here was a terrible famine in Israel. The ground was very dry, and animals were dying. There was very little food to eat. Naomi and Elimelek, her husband, had two sons. Her husband decided that they should go to another country, called Moab until the famine was over. So, they left and stayed in Moab for a very long time. Naomi's two sons got married, and she had two daughters-in-law, named Ruth and Orpah. Then, bad things started to happen.

First, Naomi's husband died, and after that, her two sons. She was left all alone in a strange land with her two daughters-in-law. She felt very sad, so she returned to Israel.

Can anything good truly come out of all these things for Naomi?

Let's read on and see.

DAY 92 – PRAYER

Thank You, God, for always helping Your people. Help those people that are in any kind of trouble. Make them know that You care for them. Help them understand that even when bad things happen, Lord, You do not leave them alone. I know, You are on my side and doing something I do not see to help me. When I am troubled, then, I will pray to You, O Lord, as You tell me to. Thank You for being with me. In Jesus' name. Amen.

DAY 93 – NAOMI DECIDES TO RETURN HOME

N aomi had left Israel with her husband and two sons for many years because of a famine. For a while, everything seemed well, but then her husband and sons all died. She was now left alone with two daughters-in-law from Moab.

What was she to do now?

Naomi decides to return home. She told her two daughters-in-law she was leaving. The first one, Orpah, kissed Naomi and went back to her people and her gods. But the second daughter-in-law, Ruth, said she wanted to go back to Israel with her.

"But I have nothing to give you," Naomi told her.

"I know, but I don't want to leave you," Ruth said. "I love you and want to be wherever you are."

"But we serve a God that is different from yours," Naomi reminded her.

"I know," said Ruth, "and I want your God to be my God and your people to be my people."

"Why?" Naomi asked.

"Because you have told us so many wonderful things about Him," Ruth said.

That made Naomi very happy, and so she and Ruth set off for Israel together.

DAY 94 – PRAYER

Thank You, dear God, for showing Your love to everyone that believes in You. Father God, please help me let my light shine by the good things I say about You and what I do. Let me tell others about You and Your great love for them. Let me do what is right so they will want to know more about You. Thank You, Father, for all Your children that will come to know You soon. In Jesus' name. Amen.

DAY 95 – RUTH MEETS BOAZ

N aomi returned to Israel, taking her daughter-in-law, Ruth, with her. Everyone was glad Naomi had come back. But Naomi was still feeling sad because she no longer had her husband and sons. She was now poor, and they did not have much food. So, she sent Ruth to gather wheat in the fields of rich farmers. That was the rule made by God for Israel. When people were rich and gathered wheat from their fields, they would purposely leave some behind for the poor people. That way, the poor people would have something to eat. Since Ruth and Naomi were poor, Ruth went out to gather some of this wheat. She stopped at Boaz's field.

Ruth was very beautiful, and Boaz asked about her. They told him that she was a very good woman who came from Moab. She was the daughter-in-law of Naomi. Boaz was very kind to Ruth and gave her a lot more wheat than she had picked up. She showed this to Naomi when she returned home. Immediately, Naomi began thinking that, maybe, God was doing something good for them both.

She would have to wait and see.

DAY 96 – RUTH FINDS A HUSBAND

Naomi was very excited when Ruth told her whose field she had stopped at to gather wheat.

"Oh, his name is Boaz, and he is a relative of my husband," she told Ruth.

Naomi told her to stay in Boaz's field for the remainder of the harvest. Every day, Boaz looked out for Ruth and even invited her to eat lunch with his people.

At the end of the harvest, there was a big party for everyone. Naomi told Ruth to go and stay near Boaz. That night, Ruth and Boaz talked, and he asked her to marry him. After a while, they were married, and Ruth was very happy. But Naomi was even happier when Ruth had a baby. She helped Ruth look after the baby. She was no longer sad, and they were no longer poor.

Indeed, God had remembered her and Ruth.

DAY 97 – ESTHER

Esther was a beautiful young girl living in Persia with her Uncle Mordecai. Her parents were dead, and he brought her up and loved her like his own child. He taught her to love and obey God at all times. He also taught her that obeying God could be very hard, but he still expected her to do the right thing.

Esther never forgot these things her uncle taught her. Then one day, something terrible happened. Some men came and took Esther away from Mordecai and into the king's palace. They were looking for a new queen, and the king sent for all the beautiful young maidens to come to the palace.

Can you imagine how Esther felt?

She was carried away to a big, strange palace with hundreds of people to meet a king she had never seen before. She and Mordecai lived not too far from the palace, so he came to see her always.

"Cheer up, Esther," he said. "You never know how God might use you because of this."

Esther did not understand what Mordecai meant. All she knew, she was scared and wanted to go back home.

What will happen to Esther in the king's palace?

Read the next story to find out.

DAY 98 – ESTHER BECOMES QUEEN

Esther found herself, along with many other girls, in the palace. They were all there to see which of them would please the king the most. Whoever did would become the Queen of Persia. Esther was a Jew, and since they were strangers in Persia, they were not liked a lot. Because of this, Mordecai told her not to tell anyone she was a Jew.

Esther did not believe for a minute that the king would choose her. After all, there were so many other girls prettier and cuter than her, or so she thought. They spent nearly a year getting themselves ready to meet with the king, one by one.

When the time came, Esther felt like she was in a beauty contest. To meet the king, all of the girls dressed up in their finest clothes and glistening diamonds. After the king met with all of them, he chose Esther to be his queen. She could hardly believe it. It felt like a dream. She, Esther, a Jew in a foreign land, was chosen to be Queen of Persia! Mordecai wondered what God had in mind for Esther as Queen of Persia.

We will find out when we read the next stories.

DAY 99 – ESTHER'S PEOPLE ARE IN BIG TROUBLE

Esther, a Jew, was now Queen of Persia. But only she and Mordecai knew she was a Jew. Many people in Persia hated the Jews because they were strangers living there. Their home was in Israel, but it was destroyed, and the Jews had scattered abroad. That's why some of them lived in Persia. A particular man in the kingdom hated the Jews and wanted to find a way to get rid of them and make some money. His name was Haman. He came up with a plan to kill all of the Jewish people who lived in the kingdom of Persia. He promised the king a lot of money if he let him do this.

The king did not know that Esther was a Jew, so he gave Haman the power to kill the Jews. Immediately, Haman made a rule that they should kill all the Jews on a particular day. That was very bad news for them, and they began to weep and pray to God to save them from this. Mordecai sent Esther a message about what Haman had planned on doing.

But she wondered, 'What can I do? I am just one person.'

Truly, what do you think Esther could do to save her people?

Read more to find out.

DAY 100 – ESTHER TAKES A BRAVE STEP

E sther, the Queen, was very worried. Her people would die on a certain day soon.

But what could she do?

She had never told anyone that she was a Jew. What would the king, her husband, say if she told him this now? It might be better not to say or do anything. But Mordecai, her uncle, told her that it would be wrong for her to keep silent. As the queen, she needed to tell the king or else all her people would die.

"Maybe, this is why God made you queen so you can save us," he said.

Esther thought about this every day. Would the king listen to her and do something?

In the kingdom, there was a rule that said no one could come before the king except he sent for them. If anyone, even the queen, came to the king without being called, he could have them killed. He had not sent for her for many days, so she would have to go to him and tell him about Haman's wicked plan.

But suppose he killed her?

After three days of prayers, without food and asking God to help her, Esther decided to go and see the king. Since he had not sent for her, she made up her mind that whatever happened, she had to do it to try and save her people.

That was a very brave thing to do.

DAY 101 – ESTHER GOES TO SEE THE KING

E sther put on her best clothes to go and see the king. She was going against the rule that said no one was to come and see the king except he sent for them. If he did not stretch out his staff towards the person, they would kill that person for daring to come before the king without an invite. She knew this, but Haman's plan against the Jews was terrible, and she needed to stop it.

Esther approached the throne with fear and trembling. Everyone was surprised that she dared to do this. They waited to see what the king was going to do. Esther waited too, breathing very hard and shaking all over, her legs wiggling and her chest going up and down. Suddenly, the king stretched out his staff.

Phew! What a relief for her?

She now knew that God had heard her prayers and was on her side. She did not tell the king right away what the problem was. Instead, she asked him to a feast so that she did not have to talk to him in front of everybody. That move was such a wise thing to do. She also invited Haman, who had planned the evil deed.

I really wonder what is going to happen at that feast.

Let's read on to find out.

DAY 102 – ESTHER SAVES HER PEOPLE

E sther was not the only person praying; so was her Uncle Mordecai and many other Jews. They knew that God loved them and would help them when they were in trouble. He was also known to give them wisdom about what to do at times like these. He gave Esther the wisdom to hold two feasts that pleased the king very much.

After the second one, the king asked her what she wanted him to do for her. Then she told him about Haman's plan to kill her people with Haman sitting right there beside the king. The king and Haman were surprised to learn that Esther was a Jew. But the king was very upset that Haman had come up with such an evil plan. If he killed all the Jews, he would be killing the king's beloved wife, too. The king told his servants to hang Haman for such an evil plan. And so, the Jews were saved by one person – dear Queen Esther, who readily laid down her life to save her people.

Mordecai was right – God had made her a queen to save her people.

DAY 103 – PRAYER

Hallelujah, God, You used one woman to save all Your people. You made Esther brave enough to go before the king. Thank You, God, for hearing and answering the prayers of Your people because You love them. I know You will do the same for me, too. Thank You once more. In Jesus' name. Amen.

DAY 104 – GOD ANSWERS HANNAH'S PRAYER

Hannah was very unhappy. She had been married for a very long time and did not have any children. Every day she prayed to God to have a child.

One day, she was in the temple praying very hard. Her lips were moving, and no words came out of her mouth. The priest thought she was drunk, but Hannah was not angry with the priest for thinking she was drunk. Instead, she said, 'No,' she was only asking God for a baby. The priest told her to go home and that God was going to answer her prayer. Nine months later, Hannah had a baby boy. She named him Samuel, which means God Has Heard. Every day she prayed to God so she could have a child.

DAY 105 – PRAYER

God, I am so glad that You answered Hannah's prayers at last. Thank You for that. You are so good at hearing us. I am going to keep on praying to You, no matter what. Lord, thank You for the many prayers You answer every day for us. In Jesus' Name. Amen.

DAY 106 – SAMUEL LEAVES HOME

Hannah had vowed to God that if He gave her a son, she would give him back to the Lord. She meant that she would let him become a servant of God in His temple at Shiloh. So, when she had Samuel, she kept him at home until she weaned the boy. Then she remembered her promise to God and took him to the temple at Shiloh. There she gave him to the priest, Eli, to teach him how to be a servant of God.

It was so hard for Hannah to leave her son and go back home, but she did anyway. Every year, she made a special coat and brought it to the temple for him. Samuel missed his mother very much, but guess what? He loved God and being in His temple. He wanted to serve and please the God who answered his mother's prayer. Eli was happy to have young Samuel around. He was so quick to learn and do the things of God.

Even a small child can serve God, and you are not too tiny.

DAY 107 – PRAYER

T hank You, God, for You always keep Your promises to us. Lord, I am learning that when we make You a promise, we must keep it. I am sure Hannah missed Samuel very much, but she kept her word. Let me learn to keep my promises to You and others. I bless Your name for being so nice to me. In Jesus' name. Amen.

DAY 108 – GOD TALKS TO SAMUEL

S amuel was only a small boy when God first talked to him.

Can you imagine that? And how did this happen?

One night, Samuel went to sleep on his little bed in his room. After he fell asleep, he heard someone calling his name.

"Samuel, Samuel," the voice said.

Samuel jumped up and rubbed his sleepy eyes. 'Who was calling him?' he wondered. He hurried over to Eli's room.

"Did you call me, Father Eli?" he asked.

"No, son, I did not. Go back to sleep."

Samuel went back to bed. The voice came another time, and he went back to Eli.

"But you did call me," Samuel said.

"No, I didn't."

So, Samuel went back to bed. The voice came the third time, and this time Eli knew it was God calling Samuel. So, he told Samuel that the next time he heard the voice, he should say, "Speak Lord, Your servant hears You."

When Samuel did this, God spoke to him. Samuel was both afraid and happy. He found out that God knew his name and had a special job for him to do in Israel.

Always remember that God knows your name, and He has a special job for you to do, too.

DAY 109 – PRAYER

Thank You, God, because You know the number of the hairs in my head. Dear God, You know my name, and I am so happy about that. It also means that You have a special job for me to do. Please help me to find it and do it well. Thank You, Lord, for having a plan for me, even before I know it. In Jesus' name. Amen.

DAY 110 – ISRAEL ASKS FOR A KING

S amuel grew up strong in the temple. Then he became a judge and prophet over Israel after Eli died. His mother was happy the child she had prayed for was now a priest of God. Samuel now taught the people to obey God.

They all knew that God was their King. He gave them the strength to fight and win their battles against their enemies. He blessed them with many good things and kept them safe. The only thing was, they could not see God. He was invisible, just as He is today. After a while, the Israelites did not like this. They looked around them and saw other nations with kings. They now wanted a man on earth to be their king instead of God. They wanted a king they could see.

They told this to Samuel. He was upset, and so was God. He did not want His people to be like those around them. If they followed them, they would do many wrong things. But since the people did not stop asking, God decided to give them a king.

Do you want to know who God chose as Israel's first king?

Read the next story to find out.

DAY 111 – PRAYER

Thank You, God, because You had made everything we needed when You created this world. God, You know that sometimes, I want something, so I keep asking You for it. Now I understand that this is not always a good thing, especially if it is something You do not want me to have. Please help me trust You with what I want and accept the answer You give me. Also, help my parents to trust in You, too. Thank You for the answer. In Jesus' name. Amen.

DAY 112 – GOD CHOOSES A KING FOR ISRAEL

G od decided to give Israel a king. But who would it be?

There was a man whose name was Kish. He had a son. He sent him to find some of his donkeys that had run away. The son and his friends traveled all over the country looking for the donkeys. But they did not find them. Hot, tired, and hungry, they came to a town where Samuel was staying.

"Let's talk to the man of God," one of them said. "Maybe, he'll know where the donkeys are," he concluded.

They found Samuel, and he prepared a special feast for them. He took a cup of oil and poured it over Kish's son's head. Then he told him that God had called him to be Israel's first king. The young man was amazed. He had left his home to look for a donkey, and he was now going back, as a king, chosen by God! His name was Saul.

That was truly amazing.

God can choose anyone to serve Him.

DAY 113 – SAUL DOES THE WRONG THING

Saul was the King of Israel for a time, and he fought and won many battles. He led the people very well. One day, the Philistines came to attack Israel. The people were so afraid that they hid in caves, in the bushes, and among the rocks. Samuel told Saul to wait until he came and made an offering to God before going into battle. Saul and the people waited for seven days, and Samuel did not come as promised. The people grew even more afraid that the Philistines would overcome them. Saul felt he had to do something since Samuel had not yet come with God's plan. So, he offered the sacrifice to God, which only Samuel should do. Soon after, Samuel came along and told Saul he had done something very wrong.

Because of this, Samuel told him he would not be King of Israel for long.

We should never let what is happening around us make us disobey God.

DAY 114 – PRAYER

Lord, thank You very much for You are always there for us. Lord, sometimes my friends make me do wrong things. Sometimes I know it is wrong, but I don't want them to be upset or leave me out of the show. I need Your help to make me say, "No," when I know what they are doing is wrong. Lord, I know You will give me the strength to say, "No," from now on. Thank You for that. In Jesus' name. Amen.

DAY 115 – SAUL DISOBEYS GOD AGAIN AND LOSES HIS CROWN

Sometimes, Saul was a good king, but other times, he was a bad one. That was because he disobeyed God more often than he obeyed Him. That was not good. Once, when Saul was fighting against the Amalekites, God told him to kill all the animals belonging to the enemies. But Saul did not do this when he defeated the Amalekites. Instead, he kept some of the best animals for himself and his soldiers. Samuel, God's prophet, was very upset with him for not obeying God's commands. So, God told Samuel to tell Saul that He would take away the kingdom from him and give it to someone else one day.

We don't win when we disobey God.

DAY 116 – PRAYER

Lord, thank You for giving someone to watch over me here on earth. Dear God, I see that things do not go well with us when we don't obey You. Please help me to learn this from now on, so I will always obey Your Word. I know when I've disobeyed my parents, they will take away my toys. If they are not happy when I do not obey them, You will not be happy either. Lord, I don't want to miss going into Your Kingdom because of my disobedience. Thank You for being with me. In Jesus' name. Amen.

DAY 117 – SAUL AND HIS SON, JONATHAN

Jonathan was the name of Saul's son. His father adored him, and he, in turn, adored his father. They went to war against the Philistines together. Jonathan trusted in the Lord to help them win the war because he believed the Lord could save either by few or many. So, Jonathan and one of the other soldiers decided to go across to the camp of their enemies, the Philistines. Jonathan and his buddy believed that God was on their side and would give them the victory. Their action was a very dangerous thing to do. To get to the Philistines, Jonathan and the other soldier climbed over some steep rocks. They called out to their enemies, and they dared them to come to their camp. Jonathan knew God was with him, so he and his friend went across and fought with the Philistines. God helped them defeat their enemies, and the Philistines ran away. Saul saw that Jonathan, his son, was a very brave young man.

He was proud of him.

DAY 118 – PRAYER

Thank you, O God, for my parents. Lord, I want my parents to be proud of me. Please help me be good, helpful, polite, and do what they tell me without talking back rudely and giving them trouble. Lord, provide them with the grace to be patient with me. Thank You for always answering me. In Jesus' name. Amen.

DAY 119 – GOD CHOOSES ANOTHER KING FOR ISRAEL

Saul kept on disobeying God. So, God decided to give the Kingdom of Israel to another king. He wanted someone who would always obey Him. Saul did not like this, but there was nothing he could do about it.

God told Samuel to go to the house of a man named Jesse. He had eight sons.

"I will show you the one you must choose to be king," He said to Samuel.

Samuel went to Bethlehem to Jesse's house. He made a feast and invited Jesse and his sons. Seven of Jesse's sons passed before Samuel, and the Lord did not pick any of them. Among them was Eliab, who was physically strong. When Samuel saw Eliab, he was like, wow! This must be him. But God told him Eliab was not the one because men look on the outside of people, but God looks at our hearts. Samuel did not know what to do.

Then he asked Jesse, "Do you have any more sons?"

"Oh, yes, there is one more, David. He's out in the field with the sheep."

"Send for him," Samuel said.

As soon as David showed up, God said to Samuel, "This is the one. Anoint him."

And so, Samuel anointed David to be the next King of Israel in the presence of his family. God had looked at David's heart and saw that it was good.

DAY 120 – DAVID, THE SONGWRITER

David was still a young boy when Samuel anointed him as king. That means he would have to wait sometime before he sat on the throne. That did not bother David at all. He liked being a shepherd. Out in the open field, he talked to God a lot. He also played his harp and made up a lot of songs to God. Here is one of the songs he wrote to God:

'O COME, let us sing to the Lord; let us make a joyful noise to the Rock of our salvation! Let us come before His presence with thanksgiving; let us make a joyful noise to Him with songs of praise!'

It is good for us to praise God with joyful singing, just like David did.

DAY 121 – PRAYER

Dear God, here is my prayer of praise. Praise You, God, because You love me. Praise You, God, because You made me. Praise You, God, because You watch over me. Praise You, God, because You gave me parents. Praise You, God, for watching over kids like me, without parents. Praise You, God, because Jesus is coming back for me! Hallelujah! In Jesus' name. Amen.

DAY 122 – DAVID THE BRAVE SHEPHERD BOY

David was a shepherd. He looked after his father's sheep. He had to stay outside, watching over them day and night. Sometimes, it was very cold, and sometimes, it was very dark. At nights, the wolves and other animals would come and try to steal the sheep. He had to fight them off.

One day, a lion came to steal a sheep. David prayed to God and asked Him to help him chase away the lion. God made David strong, so he killed the lion and saved the sheep. Another time, a bear came to take away one of the sheep. David killed it, too, by the power of God. He was a very brave young man who trusted God to help him do impossible things.

DAY 123 – DAVID AND GOLIATH

David grew up believing that with God's help, he could do anything. Now, the Israelites were fighting with the Philistines. All of David's bigger brothers had gone to the war. Because he was the smallest one, he had to stay home and look after the sheep. One day, his father sent him to carry some food for his brothers. When he got there, he was surprised to hear a loud voice saying,

"Who is coming to fight me?"

It was a very big giant named Goliath, an Israelite enemy. All of the Israelites were scared and ran away.

"Is no one going to fight him?" David asked.

"We can't," they said. "He's a giant. He'll kill us all."

"No, he won't, said David. "I'll defeat him with the help of our God."

"You're crazy," the soldiers told him.

But David kept saying he could do it. So, they told King Saul about David.

King Saul sent David to fight the giant because no one else would do it. The Philistines laughed when they saw the little boy coming to fight their giant. They were sure Goliath was going to win. But David put a very smooth stone in his sling. Round and round, he twirled it and let it go. The stone hit Goliath, "smack bang" in the middle of his forehead.

"Boof!"

Down the giant tumbled to the ground, dead. Israel rejoiced, and the Philistines ran away from them. That happened because a little boy named David believed in God.

DAY 124 – PRAYER

T hank You, dear Lord, because You can use anybody, big or small, black or white, and rich or poor. David was only a little boy, dear Father, and Goliath was a very big giant, but he was not afraid because David knew and believed in You. He trusted in You, and so he won the battle with the giant. When I have issues, please help me to be brave and trust in You. Thank You, my King, for giving me the strength to be brave. In Jesus' name. Amen.

DAY 125 – SAUL SENDS FOR DAVID

Saul was having trouble falling asleep at night. Sometimes, for no reason, he became very upset and acted up. His servants told him that listening to music would help him to sleep better. He asked his men if they could find someone who played beautiful music to help him. They told him about David, Jesse's son, a sweet singer, and played the lyre. Saul sent for him to come and live at the palace. Whenever he was feeling miserable and could not sleep, David played music for him. Then he would fall into a peaceful sleep.

God made David play beautiful music, which he used to help someone else. We should always use our talents and gifts to help others.

DAY 126 – DAVID AND JONATHAN

Jonathan was Saul's oldest son. When David came to the palace to live, they became best friends. David played music for Saul when he was feeling upset. He also went to war for him. One day, Saul and David went to war and defeated Israel's enemies. When they came back, the people danced for joy in the streets. They made up songs about David and Saul. The women sang that Saul had killed a thousand people in battle, while David killed ten thousand. When Saul heard this, he became jealous of David. So, he tried to kill him. But Jonathan warned David about this, so he got away. He still loved David as his friend and did not want anything bad to happen to him.

DAY 127 – ABIGAIL, A WISE WOMAN

Saul was always chasing David all over the place, trying to kill him. David kept going from one town to the next to get away from Saul. One of the times, he came near a sheep farm in Carmel. The shepherd's name was Nabal, and he had a lot of sheep. He was married to a wise woman named Abigail, who trusted in God.

David helped watch over Nabal's sheep in the day and at night. As time went on, David and his men became very hungry. But they did not steal any of Nabal's sheep. Instead, David sent and asked Nabal if he could give him a few sheep for food. Although Nabal had many sheep, he was very mean and said no. That made David very angry.

When Nabal's wife heard about what her husband had done to David, she knew that David might plan to kill her husband. Quickly, she got some food and sheep and hurried to meet David before he came to her home. She knelt before David and begged him not to harm her husband. She reminded him that doing this would not please God. She also told him that he would be the King of Israel one day, and he would not want people to know he had done this evil thing. David listened to her wise words and thanked her for keeping him from doing something wrong.

Abigail, a wise woman, had saved her family's lives.

DAY 128 – PRAYER

Thank You, God, for keeping me out of serious trouble. Dear God, teach me what to do when I see trouble coming for myself and others. Abigail was a wise woman of God because she had an idea of what could happen. But she did not just sit down and let it happen. She got up and did something to keep it from happening, and it worked. Help me to be like that. Thank You, for I know You will give me the wisdom to do the right things. In Jesus' name. Amen.

DAY 129 – DAVID REFUSES TO KILL SAUL

David was a man of God. Even when things went wrong, he always tried to do what was right. One of the times when he was running away from Saul, he and his men went far inside a cave to rest. While they were in there, Saul also came into the cave. He did not know that David and his men were far away in the back of the same cave.

What would you do if someone who is trying to kill you came where you were?

Well, David's men told him to kill King Saul. This way, David would become king. But David said, "No," he will not do it." He did not think God wanted him to become king this way. So, he did not kill King Saul. He came out of the cave and let Saul live. That pleased God very much because David left it up to Him to decide when he should become King of Israel.

DAY 130 – DAVID REMEMBERS HIS PROMISE

S aul died, and David became the new King of Israel after him. Everyone was very happy, for they knew that this was what God wanted. They expected David to kill all of Saul's children and grandchildren as the new king. Jonathan, one of Saul's sons, was David's best friend. But he died in battle, leaving behind his son, Mephibosheth.

Mephibosheth was lame in his feet because he fell from his nurse's hand when he was a baby. He could not walk very well after that.

When Saul, his grandfather, died, Mephibosheth lived as far away from David as he could. But David never forgot his promise to Jonathan, his best friend, to be kind to his children. One day, one of David's servants came to fetch Mephibosheth. He was very afraid. He wondered what the new king was going to do to him. When he got to the palace, David invited him to live there. Surprised, Mephibosheth asked him why. David told him that his father was his best friend, and because of that, he wanted to show him kindness.

Mephibosheth was very glad and lived at the palace with King David.

DAY 131 – PRAYER

Dear God, thank You because, just like David, You keep Your promises. It doesn't matter how long ago You made them. I like that You always keep Your promises. That makes it easy for me to trust You. Help me to be able to keep my promises to You, too. Thank You for letting me know that You are a promise keeper. In Jesus' name. Amen.

DAY 132 – DAVID LEARNS TO FORGIVE

King David was having trouble in his kingdom. Absalom, one of his sons, was trying to take his throne from him. Because of this, David had to leave Jerusalem quickly. He was going to another place to hide. On his way there, Shemiel met him. Shemiel did not like David because he became king after Saul died. When he saw David coming, he cursed him and threw stones at him. David's men were upset and told David to let them go and kill him. But David said no, he forgave him even if he was mean. He left it up to God to punish him if He wanted to do so. That was very kind of David.

DAY 133 – PRAYER

Lord, thank You for Your Word because it always tells us what is right. Oh God, Your Word says we are to bless those who curse us and do good to those who hate us. That was what David did, and it made You happy. God, I want to please You too, so I will try and do the same. Please give me a heart that pleases You. Thank You, Ancient of Days. In Jesus' name. Amen.

DAY 134 – DAVID AND GOD'S TEMPLE

David loved God so much and wanted to do everything to please Him. David ordered his singers and priests to praise God every minute of the day. They took turns doing this, so there was endless praise and worship. David made up many songs, called psalms, for the priests and people to sing when praising God. Some of them went like this:

"Make a joyful noise, everyone, come before his presence with thanksgiving. Praise God for his goodness, and mercy goes on forever. Let us sing of the goodness of the Lord forever."

Now, the place where people went to worship God was in a tent and not a house. Then David thought it would be a wonderful thing to make a house or temple for God. The prophet, Nathan, thought so, too. But then God told Nathan to tell David that his son, Solomon, should be the one to build the temple. David was disappointed that he could not do it. But he made sure he gathered all the things that Solomon would need to build a house for God.

When we love God, we always want to do something wonderful for Him.

DAY 135 – PRAYER

Oh Lord, one of the best things I can do for You is praising and worshiping You. Come on, everybody, let us worship the Lord for His goodness, love, forgiveness, kindness, and always taking care of us. I will praise You, O God. Praise ye the name of the Lord! In Jesus' name. Amen.

DAY 136 – SOLOMON CHOOSES WISDOM

Solomon became the King of Israel before David, his father, died. He was a very young man and had a large kingdom to rule. After the death of his father, he was not sure how to rule God's people well. As he thought about this, one night, God appeared to him. He told Solomon to ask Him for anything he wanted. What would you have asked for if you were Solomon? Lots of toys, cars, houses, trips and holidays, plenty of money, what? Solomon did not ask God for any of these things. Instead, he asked for wisdom to rule God's people right.

God was very pleased with Solomon's answer. God gave him wisdom, and Solomon became the wisest man in the whole world. Although he did not ask to be rich, God also made him a very rich man too. The Bible says wisdom is the best thing we could ever ask for.

DAY 137 – PRAYER

T hank You, dear Lord, for Your mercies endure forever. God, Your Word says wisdom is the best thing, and I believe You. So please give me plenty of time to be wise and do what You want me to do. Thank You because You have given me that wisdom. In Jesus' name. Amen.

DAY 138 – SOLOMON AND THE BABY

After King David died, Solomon, his son, became the next king. He was a very wise man after God gave him the wisdom that he asked for. He knew a lot of things and what to do when things went wrong. Because of this, people came from near and far to hear his wise words.

One day, two ladies came to him about a baby. The two of them lived together in a house, and each had a baby. One of the ladies' babies died during the night. She took her dead baby and put it on the bed of the other lady, who was sleeping. Then she took the live baby as her own. When the other lady woke up and saw the dead baby beside her, she knew it was not her baby, but the other lady said it was. So, they came to the king to settle the matter. The two ladies kept on saying the living baby was theirs. Then, King Solomon ordered one of his guards to bring him a sword, and he put the baby on a table and said he would cut it in two and give each one a half. One of the ladies said this was the right thing to do. The birth mother of the living baby begged King Solomon not to do it. She would rather live childless than have her baby killed.

King Solomon smiled and said, "Give the baby to this woman. She is the real mother because she does not want her baby to die."

That was a very wise thing for the king to do.

DAY 139 – PRAYER

H God, I just want to praise You because I know You are the one that gives us every good gift. My Father, teach me not to lie or cheat to get what I want. It is wrong, and it makes You sad when I do it. Help me to speak the truth even when it will get me into trouble. Thank You because I know You have answered me. In Jesus' name. Amen.

DAY 140 – A QUEEN COMES TO LEARN WISDOM

S olomon was known all over the world because of his wisdom. He knew and understood many things others did not know. So, everyone near and far came to visit him to learn from him. God says we should all seek after His wisdom because it will teach us how to please Him and live right.

A particular queen came from a faraway land, called Sheba, to visit Solomon and learn of his wisdom. She brought him many gifts, and she spent some time learning from him.

Before she left to return home, she blessed God for giving Solomon so much wisdom. Like the Queen of Sheba, we should seek wisdom so we know how to please God.

DAY 141 – PRAYER

Thank You because You are the only one that gives wisdom. You said in Your Word that if anybody lacks wisdom, he should ask for it. The Queen of Sheba came from very far to learn about You, God. She must have wanted it very much. God, please make me want to learn about You so much that I will do anything for this to happen. Thank You, dear Lord, for giving me the power to do so. In Jesus' name. Amen.

DAY 142 – A BOY BECOMES KING OF JUDAH

Josiah was just eight years of age when he became King of Judah. He was only a small boy, but he always wanted to please God. When he became king, the people were not following God's rules. That bothered him very much. The book with God's laws was lost.

One day, someone found it and brought it to the king. King Josiah sent the book to the prophetess, Huldah. She read the book and told him God would make bad things happen to the people if they did not stop disobeying His laws. Josiah was very upset to hear this. So, he made the priests teach the people how to keep the laws of God. That pleased God very much. Josiah lived a long time and brought the people back to God.

This story tells you that you are never too young to serve God.

DAY 143 – PRAYER

Lord, I thank You because You do not respect people for who they are – king, big, black, white, or kids. Dear God, it must be nice to be a king or a queen, like Josiah, but I would not know what to do. I want to be like Josiah and read your Word to find out what You want me to do and then do it. I am not an earthly king or queen, but I still want to obey Your Word. Thank You because I am a prince and princess in Your Kingdom, and I will reign with You in a short while. In Jesus' name. Amen.

DAY 144 – ELIJAH AND GOD'S DISOBEDIENT PEOPLE

There was a prophet of God whose name was Elijah. He was fearless and always spoke the truth. The children of Israel were acting up. They had stopped worshipping God and were serving a false god named Baal instead. Elijah kept telling them to come back to God because He was not happy with what they were doing. But the people did not listen. They kept serving Baal. So, Elijah told them that there would be no dew or rain in the land for a long time because they were disobeying God. Without water, the ground became very dry, and no plants could grow. The crops and animals died. There was very little food to eat. That was called a famine.

So, what do you think happened next?

Read the next story to find out.

DAY 145 – CHOOSE WHOM YOU WILL SERVE

The Israelites were disobedient to God. He sent Elijah to warn them that they should start obeying Him again. But the people would not listen even after God sent a famine on the land. There was hardly any food to eat, the plants withered, and the animals were also dying.

God loved the people of Israel and only wanted good things for them. But He could only bless them if they started to obey Him again. So, Elijah decided to hold a contest between God, and the false god named Baal, who the Israelites had gone to serve instead of God Almighty.

Hmm..., who do you think will win the contest?

Read the next story to find out.

DAY 146 – PRAYER

T hank You, God Almighty, because Your Word is yes and amen. Lord God, Your Word says You will always bless those who obey You. I want to be blessed by You, so please give me a heart that will obey You. Thank You for Your best for my life is yet to come. In Jesus' name. Amen.

DAY 147 – THE CONTEST BETWEEN JEHOVAH AND BAAL

For the contest, Elijah told the Israelites to meet him on Mount Carmel. He, Elijah, would stand in place of God, their God. They were also to bring the priests of Baal. All of the people came out, along with the priests of Baal, who were many. Whoever won the contest would be their God, Elijah told them.

For the contest, the priests of Baal and Elijah would call on their god by offering a sacrifice. The god that answered by fire – brought fire from Heaven and burnt up the sacrifice, would be the true God to worship.

Who do you think is the real God that will send down fire and burn up the sacrifice?

Let's find out in the next story.

DAY 148 – PRAYER

Thank You, God, because I know You are the only true God to worship because You alone made the heavens, earth, and everything in it. Let me never become like the Israelites who stopped believing in You. May I love and worship You forever. Thank You for living forever. In Jesus' name. Amen.

DAY 149 – WHO WINS – BAAL OR JEHOVAH?

The disobedient children of God were not sure who would win the contest. They watched as the priests of Baal built an altar and put the body of a cow on it. Then the priests began to call on Baal to send down fire from Heaven and burn up the cow. They called out loudly to Baal, cut themselves with knives until blood gushed out, leaped up and down for a very long time. But nothing happened.

"Baal is probably sleeping or on a journey," Elijah mocked them.

Then they yelled even louder, with no result.

The time for Baal's servants was up, and the fire did not come down from Heaven.

Now, it was Elijah's turn. He built an altar unto God and put a cow on it, too. Elijah also poured a lot of water on the animal and into the trench. You and I know that water puts out fire. So, it would be a tough thing for the wet offering to catch fire. Then Elijah prayed. He did not run around and jump all over the place as the priests of Baal had done. He just said a simple prayer, and immediately, fire came down from Heaven and burned up the offering on the altar. The Israelites were frightened and fell on their faces. Now, they all knew that Jehovah was the only true God, and they went back to worshipping Him.

Even so, we should worship Jehovah, the only true God, too.

DAY 150 – PRAYER

Lord God, I worship and praise You. You are the only true God. I bow down before You and honor Your greatness, for You are good, and Your kindness to us goes on forever. I will sing praises to You forever. I bless Your name, O God. In Jesus' name. Amen.

DAY 151 – ELIJAH, THE MIGHTY RUNNER

Now, as soon as the people agreed to go back to worshipping God as the one true God, something happened. God decided to send them rain so there would be no more famine on the land. Elijah prayed for the rain to come. He prayed seven times before dark clouds appeared in the sky and strong winds began to blow.

Then he went to Ahab, the King of Israel, and said, "Hurry home because a lot of rain is going to fall soon."

The king set off quickly in his chariot to get home before the heavy rains started.

But guess what?

Elijah started running, too, and he ran so fast, by the power of God, that he got back to Jerusalem before the king in his chariot. That was some amazing running.

If Elijah did that today, he would be a super athlete!

DAY 152 – PRAYER

Father God, You made Elijah run so very fast that he outran a horse. You can make us hop, skip, jump and do so many other things. Thank You, God, for giving us a body, our hands, feet, and everything else so we can do all the fun things we enjoy. In Jesus' name. Amen.

DAY 153 – ELIJAH IS HUNGRY

Before Elijah met with the priests of Baal on Mount Carmel, the famine had been going on for a long time. The people were starving most of the time because they had very little food to eat. God told Elijah to go and live beside a small river at Cherith. There he got water to drink, and every day God sent birds to bring him bread and meat.

That was how God kept Elijah alive during the famine in Israel.

But guess what?

One day, the river dried up, and the birds no longer brought Elijah food. What was he going to do now? Would God let his servant die from hunger and thirst?

We'll find out in the next story.

DAY 154 – PRAYER

F ather God, I want to tell You thanks because You give us food to eat every day. I do not have to worry about going hungry. I love to eat all the nice things You have supplied. I want to pray for the kids that do not have much food to eat. Lord, they will be sad and sometimes cry when they are hungry. Help them in Your way, O God. Thanks for giving us our food every day. In Jesus' name. Amen.

DAY 155 – ELIJAH AND THE WIDOW

E lijah no longer had any water to drink or food to eat. He wondered what he was to do now. Then God told him to go to a town called Zarephath, where a widow would feed him. When he got there, he saw the widow gathering some sticks to make a fire. He begged her for some food. The woman told him she only had enough food to make a meal for herself and her son. Elijah asked her just to bake a little cake for him first. That was a tough thing for the widow to do. If she gave Elijah a cake, she would have very little left for herself and her son. But she was a kind woman who believed in God and helping others. So, she went and baked the cake for Elijah first.

After he ate it, he told her that she would always have food in her house for the rest of the famine. God blessed her for her kindness to Elijah, a servant of God. She always had food in her home, just like Elijah told her.

Praise God!

DAY 156 – PRAYER

Thank You, God, for You always bless us for our kindness to others. But even if You don't do it right away, God, it gives us a good feeling when we help others. That is one way of showing our love to others. Please help me be kinder to others so I can be like the widow who had little but still gave out of the small amount she had. Thank You for making me a giver. In Jesus' name. Amen.

DAY 157 – ELIJAH BRINGS THE WIDOW'S SON BACK TO LIFE

E lijah had to stay with the widow and her son during the famine. Because of God's blessing, they always had food during the famine in Israel.

One day, the widow's son fell ill, and he died. The widow was heartbroken about this, and so was Elijah. So, he took the boy's body up to his room and laid him on the bed. Then Elijah prayed to God on high and asked Him to make the widow's son live again because she had been so good to him. God heard Elijah's prayer and made the boy come alive again.

Everyone was happy and praised God for this miracle.

DAY 158 – PRAYER

Dear God, I want to praise You because You answer prayers about big and small things. That was certainly a huge thing, but still, You did it. Thank You for Your mighty power, O God. In Jesus' name. Amen.

DAY 159 – GOD PROMISES TO TAKE ELIJAH TO HEAVEN

M any people don't believe there is a place called Heaven, but the Bible talks about it all the time. Heaven is the place where God lives with His angels. We cannot find our way to Heaven. Only God can take us there. Only the people who love God, believe in Jesus from their hearts, and confess with their mouth that God raised Him from the dead get to go to Heaven to live with Him. Jesus also promises us that one day we will be in Heaven with Him. But most of us have to die before we can go there. But a few people get to go to Heaven while they are still alive. Elijah was one of these men.

When his work on earth was over, God told him that He would take him to Heaven while he was still alive.

Can you imagine how excited and happy Elijah was to hear this? He could hardly wait for the day to come.

We'll tell you exactly how it happened in the next story.

DAY 160 – PRAYER

Dear Lord, thank You for making that place called Heaven. Your Word has said so many beautiful things about it. God, I believe that Heaven is a real place, and I want to go there one day. Jesus says He is there preparing a place for me. Help me remain faithful to You so that He will take me there with Him when He comes back. Thank You for that beautiful place. In Jesus' name. Amen.

DAY 161 – ELIJAH GOES TO HEAVEN

E lijah was a very powerful prophet of God who worked many miracles. He was very excited because God had promised to take him up to Heaven alive. He did not know exactly when, so he and his servant, Elisha, went for a long walk.

"You know I am going to be taken up to Heaven today," Elijah said to Elisha.

"Yes, I know," replied Elisha.

"Is there anything you want from me before I go?" Elijah asked him.

Elijah was not a rich man. But there was something he had that Elisha wanted very much.

"Yes, my Lord," he said. "I want to be even more powerful than you are as a prophet."

Elijah was pleased to hear this. He said, "If you see me when I am taken up into Heaven, then you will have your prayer answered."

Elisha was glad, and so wherever Elijah went, he followed behind him. As they were walking, suddenly, a fiery chariot appeared from Heaven. Before Elisha could do or say anything, he saw Elijah caught up to Heaven in the chariot.

Then he disappeared. Elisha wished he could have gone with him, but he knew he could not. Then he looked around and saw Elijah's coat on the ground. He picked it up, and when he came to the river, he used it to hit the water. To his surprise, a dry path opened up in the river, and he passed through it. Elisha knew this was a miracle and that he now had power like his master, Elijah.

DAY 162 – PRAYER

Dear God, thank You for Your works that leave me in awe every day. You always amaze me with them; then, I have to open my mouth wide and say, "Wow!" Elijah was so blessed, Father. He went to Heaven without dying. What a wonder! Because You took him there, I know I will get there one day. I can't wait to see Jesus, the angels, the horses, the streets of gold, and the other beautiful things You say are there. Keep me true to You, Lord, so that I will make it there. Thank You for being there for me. In Jesus' name. Amen.

DAY 163 – ELISHA BECOMES THE NEW PROPHET

N ow that Elijah was taken up to Heaven by God, Elisha became the new prophet. Many young men followed Elisha so he could teach them how to be prophets of God.

One day, Elisha and the prophets' trainees came to a city and decided to live there. The city's water was not good for drinking, and the ground did not grow many crops for food. The people told this to Elisha, and he did something strange. He took salt, threw it into the water, and made it good for drinking, and the ground became fruitful.

That was a miracle and showed the people that he was indeed a man of God.

DAY 164 – THE OIL IN THE BARREL

N ow, one of Elisha's followers died, leaving behind his wife and children. The dead man owed someone a lot of money, and his wife could not pay him back when he came for it. He decided he would have to take away her children and sell them to get back his money. The widow did not want to lose her children, so she ran to Elisha and told him her problem.

"What do you have in your house?" Elisha asked her.

"All I have is one pot of oil," she said.

"Well, this is what you must do," he told her. "Go borrow all the empty pots and pans you can get from your neighbors. Then take them home and lock your door, then start pouring oil from that pot into all the empty pans."

That did not make sense to the lady, but she did as Elisha told her.

And guess what?

The one pot of oil became many as she poured from it until she filled all the empty pans. Then she sold the oil and made enough money to pay her bills and look after her family.

That was indeed a miracle from God.

DAY 165 – PRAYER

Lord, thank You for Your miracles. Sometimes, what You tell us to do, dear Father does not seem to make sense. But this story teaches me that I must trust You, and You will work things out. It is so good to know this. I praise You, God. In Jesus' name. Amen.

DAY 166 – THE KIND WOMAN

As the prophet of God, Elisha traveled all over Israel to deliver God's message to His people. He also helped them with their problems, and, sometimes, he worked miracles to do this.

One day, a Shunammite woman saw him passing, and she invited him to come into her house and have something to eat. From then on, whenever she saw him passing by, she would invite him inside for a meal. She knew very well that Elisha was a man of God, and she loved being kind to him.

Then one day, she told her husband that they should build a room for Elisha in their house, and her husband agreed. The next time Elisha came by, they showed him the room and told him he would stay with them whenever he came their way. Elisha was very thankful to them for a place to rest and for the food they gave him. He also thanked God very much for making this woman and her husband so kind to him.

DAY 167 – PRAYER

T hank You, heavenly Father, for the many kind people
I meet. Some of them are my friends and family, but
some, I do not know. They will see me with my mom and
dad at the grocery store or some other place and wave at
me to make me happy. Lord God, help those people to know
and love You if they don't. Help me also to show kindness to
others, too. Thank You for the answer, dear Lord. In Jesus'
name. Amen.

DAY 168 – ELISHA SAYS THANK YOU IN ANOTHER WAY

E lisha was very thankful for the woman and her husband's kindness to him. Whenever he passed their way, he had a room to sleep in and a good meal to eat. He wanted to show them special thanks for their kindness. So, he asked his servant, Gehazi, if he knew anything that the woman and her husband would want as a thank you gift. Gehazi told him that they had everything they needed, except for one thing. They did not have a child. Elisha was glad to hear this, and so he called the woman and told her that she would have a baby soon. The woman did not believe him because she had stopped praying for this to happen. But Elisha was a man of God, and God answered his prayers. The following year, a beautiful baby boy was born to the woman and her husband, and they were all very happy.

DAY 169 – PRAYER

Lord, thank You for when I ask You something, You always answer me. Elisha asking You, God, to let the woman have a baby was really cool. She and her husband must have been so happy. Help me to know that I can pray for others too, and You will answer me. Now, I just want to pray for all the new babies born now that You will guide and protect them and their moms, O God. Whoa! Did you hear that, Mom and Dad? I prayed for people I did not know. I bless Your name, my Father in Heaven because I know You just answered my prayer. In Jesus' name. Amen.

DAY 170 – A BOY COMES BACK TO LIFE

In the previous story, we saw where Elisha prayed for the Shunammite woman, and she and her husband had a son. The boy was their only son, and they loved him very much.

One day, he went out into the fields to work with his father. His head began to hurt him, and he became ill. They quickly took him home to his mother, and before the day was over, he died. You can imagine how sad this made his parents. Their only son was dead. But his mother believed in God and that He could bring their son back to life again. So, she rode a donkey very quickly to where Elisha lived and told him what had happened.

Elisha hurried back with her and went alone into the room where the dead child was lying on the bed. He prayed and asked God to bring him back to life. Then the child sneezed, "Achoo! Achoo!" seven times and sat up. He was alive!

His parents were happy and gave thanks to God for the miracle.

DAY 171 – ELISHA WORKS MIRACLES

E lisha was teaching some young men how to be God's prophets. They lived together in the same place. One day, one of them went to gather vegetables for making soup. By mistake, he picked a poisonous plant and put it into the pot. When they were eating, they saw the plant.

"We're all going to die," they said.

But Elisha got some cornmeal and threw it into the pot. That took the poison out of the food. It could no longer hurt them. They all had a good meal, and nobody got sick or died. That was all because of the miracle-working power of Elisha, the man of God.

DAY 172 – PRAYER

My Father in Heaven, I worship Your name for this beautiful day You have made. God, when we know You, You give us the power to do incredible things. Oh God, there is no one else in the whole universe who can do these marvelous things. That's why You are God, and I will always praise You for Your good works. In Jesus' name. Amen.

DAY 173 – NAAMAN'S LITTLE MAID

Once, a little Israelite girl was captured by the soldiers and taken to their country. There she became a maid to the leader of the army and his wife. Every day the little girl saw her mistress looking sad or crying. The little girl felt sorry for her and asked her mistress what was wrong. The mistress told her that her husband had a very bad skin disease. If it did not get better soon, he was going to die.

The little maid thought about this for a while. She felt sorry for her mistress and her husband. Then she said to her, "If your husband were in my country, Israel, I know someone who could make him better."

"You mean that?" the mistress asked.

"Yes, I do. There is a man named Elisha, and he is a prophet of our God. He can make sick people better."

Her mistress told her husband, who hurried to Israel to see Elisha, the prophet of God. When he came back, his sickness was gone. Elisha, the man of God, had healed him.

Thanks to the little girl's kindness.

DAY 174 – PRAYER

Thank You, O God, because even if I am a kid, You are with me. Lord, I am not too small or too young to tell others about You. Let me not be afraid to do it, although sometimes it is hard. You tell us that everywhere we go, we must tell others about You. Please help me to do this from now on. Thank You, my Savior, for giving me the right words to say. In Jesus' name. Amen.

DAY 175 – NAAMAN BATHES IN A DIRTY RIVER TO GET CLEAN

Here's what happened when Naaman went to Israel to get healed. He filled his chariot with gold, silver, beautiful clothes, and other things as gifts for the King of Israel. But when Naaman told the king he came to be healed of his sickness, the king was afraid. When Elisha heard about Naaman, he asked the king to send Naaman to him, and the king did. Elisha's servant, Gehazi, told him Naaman was outside his door; he sent a message to Naaman saying, "Go, dip yourself seven times in the River Jordan, and you will receive your healing."

Naaman was furious. Why should he go and bathe in a dirty river when he had better ones in his country? And why did the prophet not come out to see him? Did he know that he was the captain of his king's guards? He drove away, angrily, to go back to his country.

Then one of his servants said, "Sir, if the prophet had asked you to do a great thing, would you have done it?"

Naaman said, "Yes."

"Then why don't you just do this small thing and see what happens?" asked his servant.

So Naaman stopped being angry and went down to the Jordan River. He went into the water and dipped one time.

Nothing happened. He did it again and again. He now had one more time to do it. Then, he dipped in the river for the seventh time. When he came up, the disease had disappeared from his skin.

Hallelujah!

DAY 176 – PRAYER

Thank You, dear God, for You are our Lord and God, and You can do anything. I want to tell You thanks for the beautiful things, big and small, that You do for me every day. Thank You, King of Glory, for keeping me alive and letting so many good things happen to me. In Jesus' name. Amen.

DAY 177 – GREEDY GEHAZI

G ehazi watched as Naaman took out a lot of money and clothes to pay Elisha for healing him.

'He would love to have some of that,' he reasoned.

But Elisha did not take it. So, the captain drove off in his chariot. Gehazi thought Elisha was foolish not to take the gifts Naaman offered to him. Well, if Elisha did not want them, he did.

He crept out of the house and went after Naaman. He caught up with Naaman and told him that Elisha had changed his mind about the gifts. He said Naaman should send him some clothes and money. Naaman happily gave them to him.

When Gehazi got back home, Elisha asked him where he had gone. He lied and said he had not left the house. Elisha was a prophet and knew where he had been.

He said to him, "Because you took the money and clothes from Naaman, you will get his disease also."

Gehazi was frightened. Then he looked at his hands and saw the ugly spots on them just like Naaman had before he was healed. He made one loud scream and ran from the room.

He was sorrowful for being so greedy and for telling a lie. But it was too late now.

DAY 178 – AN AXE THAT SWIMS

I ron is very heavy. If you throw it in water, it quickly sinks to the bottom. Well, one day, one of Elisha's students borrowed an iron ax and went into the woods to cut down some trees. He wanted to use the wood to help build a house. While chopping the tree, the ax's steelhead slipped off, and it fell into a deep river. He had lost the ax. What was he going to do now? He ran to Elisha and told him what had happened.

"I'm in big trouble because the ax is not mine," the student said.

"Don't worry," Elisha told him. "I'll get it back for you."

When they came to the river, Elisha asked him, "Where did the ax fall?"

The young man showed him. Then he cut a stick and threw it into the river. Immediately, the heavy iron ax swam to the top of the water, and the student picked it up.

Wow! That was a very cool miracle!

DAY 179 – ELISHA FEEDS HIS ENEMIES

Israel's enemies were always fighting against them. They did not like it that they were God's special people. Once, a very large number of Syrian soldiers came to fight Israel. The Israelites were very afraid and came to Elisha to help them. But Elisha was not afraid. He knew very well that God was on their side, and if they did what God told them, they would win the battle.

Elisha always told the King of Israel the Syrian's plans, and they did not like it. One day, the Syrians came to capture Elisha for being a tattletale for the Israelites. So, Elisha prayed that God would make all the Syrian soldiers blind, and God answered his prayer. Because they could not see, Elisha led them into the middle of Israel.

God opened the eyes of the Syrians, and now they were very afraid when they saw they were in the middle of Israel. The Israelites were happy because now they could kill all of their enemies. But Elisha told the Israelites to give them food to eat. Then, Elisha sent them back home after they finished eating.

Jesus said we should feed our enemies and treat them kindly. The Syrians were so glad to get back home safely, they stopped fighting Israel for a while.

DAY 180 – PRAYER

Lord God, thank You because You are always kind to me. God, You tell us to treat with kindness those who don't like us. Here is Elisha doing just that. The soldiers must have been surprised; we would be, too. Help me show love, not just to my friends, but also to those who don't like me. Lord, I thank You so much for giving me the grace to do just like Elisha. In Jesus' name. Amen.

DAY 181 – GOD CHASES AWAY ISRAEL'S ENEMIES

Another time, the Syrians were waging war with Israel. No one could leave Jerusalem. Their enemies surrounded the city, and soon, the Israelites did not have much water or food left. That meant that the people would start dying soon. But they kept praying to God to help them. God told Elisha that He would chase away their enemies and soon have lots of food. Some of the Israelites did not believe this because they did not know where so much food could come from.

There were four men outside the city gates. They had a disease, and they were not allowed to enter the city so that others would not catch it. The four men were very hungry. So, they decided to go over to the Syrians' camp and beg for food. They were not scared; they could have been killed. These men knew they would die of hunger anyway if they stayed behind. So off they went.

When they got there, they were surprised. The camp was empty, and there was lots of food everywhere. You see, God had made the camp hear a noise like many chariots and a great army coming at them. That made the Syrians very afraid, and they ran away, leaving everything behind. The four men went and told the people in Jerusalem, and they all came out and picked up all the food they ever wanted.

Once more, God had kept His promise to His people.

DAY 182 – PRAYER

Dear God, thank You because You are always ready to fight for us when we trust in You. That is so good to know. You are a mighty warrior for us. I will trust You to help me when I get into trouble with others. Thank You for keeping me out of trouble. In Jesus' name. Amen.

DAY 183 – ELISHA'S LAST MIRACLE

E lisha was such a mighty man of God that he was still doing miracles even after he died. How could this happen? Well, Elisha died, and they buried him in a tomb.

One day, some of the Israelites were going to bury one of their friends near Elisha's grave. On their way, they saw some of their enemies coming to get them. They were so afraid that they quickly let the dead man down into Elisha's grave. As the dead man's body touched the bones of Elisha, the dead man came to life again!

Yes, that is the power of God at work! There is nothing like that in the whole world.

DAY 184 – PRAYER

G od, Your power is the greatest in the world. No one or god is as mighty as You are. You are the only true God. May You live and rule over us forever. Thank You, our great God. In Jesus' name. Amen.

DAY 185 – DANIEL SAYS NO TO FOOD

Daniel was a Hebrew prince who was taken away to Babylon to live in Nebuchadnezzar's palace. He really missed his home and family very much. Luckily for him, he had three Israelites friends with him, so they comforted each other.

In Babylon, there were all kinds of fancy foods to eat. But Daniel and his friends remembered God's law about which food they were to eat. Most of the food they served in the palace was on the list of foods they were not supposed to eat. What were Daniel and his friends to do? Eat the food and disobey God? Not eat the food and make Nebuchadnezzar angry with them and even kill them? They decided to obey God and only have the foods God told them to eat.

They kindly asked to be given only vegetables to eat and water to drink. The servant warned them that they would be in trouble if they became ill after eating that food. Daniel and his friends trusted God to keep them healthy because they were obeying Him. After ten days, Nebuchadnezzar's servants found out that the four Hebrew boys were healthier and smarter than the rest of the boys that ate the king's food.

When we obey God, He works things out for us.

DAY 186 – THREE BOYS IN THE FIRE

N ow, Daniel's three friends were Shadrach, Meshach, and Abednego. They lived in Babylon, but they still worshipped Jehovah, the God of Israel. The Babylonians did not like this at all. They wanted them to worship their gods instead. King Nebuchadnezzar came up with a horrible idea. He built a huge statue in the middle of a plain. Then he called all the people in his kingdom together. He told them that they should bow down and worship the statue whenever they heard the music playing. To do this was wrong for Shadrach and his two friends. Their God, Jehovah, had told them not to worship any other god. So, when the music played, they did not bow down.

Nebuchadnezzar was very angry with them. He told his guards to tie them up and throw them into the furnace of fire. They threw Shadrach, Meshach, and Abednego into the fire. The King was so surprised when he saw four men walking in the fire. One was like the Son of God. He told the three Hebrews boys to come out of the fire. When they walked out, the fire had not burned them even though the people that threw them into the fire died from the flames' heat.

God kept them safe because they obeyed and trusted His Word. What a wonderful God we serve!

DAY 187 – PRAYER

Lord, thank You for Your wonderful deeds. God, You were in the middle of the fire with these three men. You came to help them when others tried to kill them. That makes me know that You are there to help me when I am in trouble. Lord, I want to thank You for always being with me in the good and the bad times. In Jesus' name. Amen.

DAY 188 – DANIEL IN THE LION'S DEN

D aniel was made a chief ruler in Babylon by Darius, the King. The Babylonians hated this because Daniel was an Israelite and a stranger. That made them think of a way to get rid of him so he would no longer rule over them. These men told the king to make a rule that no one was to pray to any god in the kingdom for thirty days, only the king. They knew that Daniel would break this rule because he always prayed three times daily to God. So King Darius made the rule, "No one should pray to any other god except me!" What a rule! Will he even know if people are praying to him?

Well, these evil men watched Daniel so they could see what he would do. Then they caught him praying and brought him to the king.

Darius, the king, loved Daniel and did not want to hurt him, but he couldn't go back on his rule. Also, the men said he had to punish Daniel for breaking the rule. Sadly, the king had Daniel thrown into the lion's den.

The Babylonian men were very happy at this. The next day, the king and these men hurried to the lions' den to see what had happened to Daniel. They were surprised to see that Daniel was alive. God Almighty had sent His angels to close the lions' mouths so they could not harm him. The king knew that the men were jealous of Daniel and wanted him dead. He became very angry and had them thrown into the lions' den after pulling Daniel out.

DAY 189 – PRAYER

Lord God, thank You for always doing a miracle in my life. God, Daniel was faithful to You. When Daniel got in trouble for doing what was right before You, You were right there to save him. He kept Your Word; he prayed every day, and he did what was right. Let me remember this and do the same things. Thank You, God, for giving me a good memory. In Jesus' name. Amen.

DAY 190 – JONAH, THE RUNAWAY PROPHET

J onah was a true prophet of God in Israel. God gave him messages, and he told them to the people.

One day, God gave a message to Jonah. God told Jonah that He was going to destroy their enemies who lived in the city of Nineveh. Jonah was glad to hear this. The people in Nineveh would not bother them anymore. But God was not finished yet. He told Jonah to go to Nineveh and tell them that He would not destroy their country if they stopped doing bad things. Now, Jonah did not like this part of the story. He wanted God to punish them. So, he decided not to go. Instead, he went on a ship that was going to another place.

God was not happy with Jonah for disobeying Him. He sent a great storm, and the sailors threw Jonah into the sea. A big fish swallowed him. Jonah knew it was God who had sent the storm and the fish. He stayed in the fish's belly for three days. Jonah was so afraid. He cried out to God, told Him he was sorry for running away and that he would go to the people of Nineveh and give them His message. God was pleased to hear this, so He let the fish vomit him up on the shores.

Immediately, Jonah set off for Nineveh.

DAY 191 – PRAYER

Lord God, You have been so good to me even when I disobey my parents, whom You have placed to care for my needs here on earth. God, I now know that it is not good to try and disobey You. Bad things can happen to me, and I will still need to come back to You for help. Please teach me how to obey You from the first time You tell me to do something. Thank You for the answer. In Jesus' name. Amen.

DAY 192 – JONAH GOES TO NINEVEH

"Whew!"

Jonah was messy and stinky when he came up out of the belly of the big fish. He was now ready to go to Nineveh with God's message. When he got there, he told the king that God was going to destroy his country. The king was terrified. He asked Jonah if there was anything he could do to stop this from happening. Jonah told him that if the people told God, they were sorry and started to do the right things, he would not destroy them. Immediately, the king told everybody to stop acting up and pray to God to forgive them. The people obeyed the king and began praying. While they were praying, all of them, and even their animals, stopped eating. God heard their prayers and saved the people and their city.

DAY 193 – PRAYER

Lord, thank You, for You are a God who answers our prayers. You invite us to come and pray to You. You said You will always hear and answer us. That is good to know that we can come to You about anything. You are a wonderful God and Father. In Jesus' name. Amen.

DAY 194 – THE SINGERS DEFEAT ISRAEL'S ENEMIES

There was a king in Judah named Jehoshaphat. He was a very good king because he always feared and obeyed God. One day, some people came to fight against Israel. The Israelites were afraid and went to the king to help them. Jehoshaphat was also afraid, but he remembered God had promised to help them whenever they called upon Him. So, Jehoshaphat fasted and prayed to God for help.

God heard his prayer, and He told them, "Fear not, I am going to fight this battle for you."

Then God told Jehoshaphat to send the choir before the army into battle. They were to sing and praise God as they went out to war. That was a bizarre thing to do, but the king obeyed what God told him to do. When the enemies of Israel heard the people singing, they became confused, started fighting each other, and ran away. That was how God defeated Israel's enemies for them.

The Israelites praised God, even more when they returned from the battle.

DAY 195 – PRAYER

Thank You, dear God, because I want to sing praises to You, my God. I want to play my music for You, O Lord. I want to beat the drums, clash the cymbals, shake my tambourine and sing aloud about Your goodness and Your love for me. Hallelujah! In Jesus' name. Amen.

DAY 196 – NEHEMIAH GETS HIS WISH

N ehemiah was a Jew living in Persia, where he was a servant to the king. His job was to pour out wine and hand it to the king to drink. But Nehemiah was very sad because the walls of his city, Jerusalem, were broken down. He longed to go back home and rebuild the city's walls and repair the temple so his people could worship God once again. But to do this, he had to get the king's permission. He was afraid to ask the king who could order him killed for doing so.

Nehemiah prayed and asked God not to let the king be angry with him. God answered his prayers, and when he asked the king, he told Nehemiah he could take some time to go back home and rebuild the walls of his city, Jerusalem.

God answered Nehemiah's prayer, but this was only the beginning. Much more had to happen before Nehemiah could build back the walls of Jerusalem.

DAY 197 – PRAYER

Thank You, God, because You always listen to me whenever I ask something of You. Dear God, sometimes I am afraid to ask for what I want. I feel shy, or I don't know what the person is going to say. Please help me to be like Nehemiah. He prayed to You, and then he asked the King for what he wanted, and he got it! Let me never be shy in asking You for anything because You are my heavenly Father. Thank You for making me Your child. In Jesus' name, amen.

DAY 198 – NEHEMIAH IS OBEDIENT AND WISE

Nehemiah was happy. The king gave him permission to go back to his country and build the city walls. The king was also very kind. He gave Nehemiah all the wood and other things he needed to build the walls. Nehemiah was also very wise. He knew that some people would not believe that the king had sent him back. So, he also asked the king for a letter to tell the other people that he had his permission to build back the walls. It was a very good thing he did this.

When he got back to Jerusalem, just as he thought, some people did not believe that the king had sent him. They thought he had come to make trouble. But when he showed them the king's letter, they knew he was speaking the truth.

That shows us that you must not only be obedient, but you must also know how to be wise.

DAY 199 – PRAYER

Thank You. Lord, for all You have done for me. Lord, sometimes I foolishly act because I am not wise. I don't always know what to do, when to do it and how to do it. Because of this, I am asking You, dear Father, to make me wise. You promised to give wisdom to anyone who asks You for it, so I know You will give it to me. Thank You because I know You will help me to believe in Your promises. In Jesus' name. Amen.

DAY 200 – NEHEMIAH HAS A PROBLEM

E ven though Nehemiah showed the other people the letter from the king, some people were still mad at him. They did not like the Jews, and they did not want them to build back their city. Two of these men were Sanballat and Tobias. First, they laughed at Nehemiah for trying to do God's work by building back the city's walls. Then when Nehemiah and his people did not stop, they tried to fight them and scare them off. But Nehemiah was very wise. He made some of the Jews keep watch while some did the work. This way, the Jews finished the wall and had a party afterward to thank God for letting them do it.

When doing something for God, we should never let others make us stop or give up.

CONCLUSION

Thank you for completing this Old Testament story-book. We are so excited you made it to the end. We must continue with the New Testament, following God all year long. God has so much for us to know yet – about Him, His plans for us, our families, and everyone.

In this book, we learned that God was there in the beginning and that He created everything. We met many Old Testament heroes like Noah, Abraham, Joseph, Moses, Samson, Esther, and King David. We learned about man's origin, the first sin, how God dealt with evil, and the beginning of the world's different nations. We also learned how to connect with God in prayer and have a one-on-one conversation with Him as our Heavenly Father.

This book of Biblical stories comprises 200 days of devotions for your family. We have a coloring book, '113 Old Testament Amazing Moments: Pointing Your Children To God Coloring Book', to go along with it. Happy coloring!

The New Testament bedtime storybook is also a stand-alone book containing 165 daily devotions of either story or prayer days. In there, you will learn how angels visited Mary and Zacharias, how Jesus took shelter in Egypt, about Paul, an enemy of Christians who later became one of them, and so much more! We also have a coloring book for our stories of the New Testament. Please consider purchasing our New Testament book from Amazon or any participating stores nearby because we want to share so much more with you about God's love and His truths for us.

This book is the very first in a series for children. The next will be for children eight years and older, and it has stories and prayers for the same day, meaning with that book, we will be praying every day. We encourage you to purchase the other one. Check our Amazon store, and you will find ways we can help you in your walk with God – every day.

We would love to see many other children being taught God's truths in their homes. If we were valuable to you in that way, please leave an honest review on Amazon or your book store, and other parents will be encouraged to teach their children about God – with our help.

God bless you in Jesus' name. Amen!

Only One Life!

RESOURCES

Children's Learning Adventure. (2019, November 18). How Repetition Helps Children Learn. Childrenslearningadventure.Com. Retrieved September 10, 2021, from

Youvesion. (1996). [Computer software]. Life Church.